Breads

CYNTHIA SCHEER
Writer and Food Stylist

JOHN P. CARROLL
Pastry Consultant

LINDA HINRICHS
CAROL KRAMER
Designers

ALLAN ROSENBERG
Major Photographer

SANDRA GRISWOLD
Photographic Stylist

ALLEN V. LOTT
Assistant Photographer

CALIFORNIA
CULINARY
ACADEMY

Ortho Books

Publisher
Robert L. Iacopi

Editorial Director
Min S. Yee

Managing Editors
Jim Beley
Anne Coolman
Susan Lammers
Michael D. Smith
Sally W. Smith

Production Director
Ernie S. Tasaki

Editors
Richard H. Bond
Alice E. Mace

System Manager
Christopher Banks

System Consultant
Mark Zielinski

Asst. System Managers
Linda Bouchard
William F. Yusavage

Photographic Director
Alan Copeland

Photographers
Laurie A. Black
Richard A. Christman

Asst. Production Manager
Darcie S. Furlan

Associate Editor
Jill Fox

Production Editors
Don Mosley
Anne Pederson

Chief Copy Editor
Rebecca Pepper

Photo Editors
Kate O'Keeffe
Pam Peirce

National Sales Manager
Charles H. Aydelotte

Sales Associate
Susan B. Boyle

Operations Assistant
Gail L. Davis

Administrative Assistant
Georgiann Wright

Address all inquiries to:
Ortho Books
Chevron Chemical Company
Consumer Products Division
575 Market Street
San Francisco, CA 94105

Copyright © 1985
Chevron Chemical Company
All rights reserved under
international and Pan-American
copyright conventions.

First Printing in July, 1985

1 2 3 4 5 6 7 8 9

85 86 87 88 89 90

ISBN: 0-89721-061-1

Library of Congress Catalog Card
Number: 85-070883

Chevron Chemical Company
575 Market Street, San Francisco, CA 94105

Danielle Walker *(left)* is chairman of the board and founder of the California Culinary Academy. **Cynthia Scheer** *(right)* is a San Francisco area based food writer and home economist whose interest in breads began with her first job after graduation from Michigan State University—a stint with the Wheat Flour Institute, a Chicago trade association devoted to encouraging home baking. She has been a food editor of *Sunset* magazine and has written 15 cookbooks. Her other books in the California Culinary Academy series include *Affordable Elegant Meals, Salads, Breakfasts & Brunches,* and *Soups & Stews.* **John P. Carroll**, who wrote pages 88 through 103 (doughnuts, brioches, croissants, and Danish pastry), is a San Francisco writer, cook, and specialist in American baking.

The California Culinary Academy Among the forefront of American institutions leading the culinary renaissance in this country, the California Culinary Academy in San Francisco has gained a reputation as one of the most outstanding professional chef training schools in the world. With a teaching staff recruited from the best restaurants of Western Europe, the California Culinary Academy educates students from around the world in the preparation of classical cuisine. The recipes in this book were created in consultation with the chefs of the California Culinary Academy.

Special thanks to:
Nell Twomey and Judith Anderson Twomey,
San Francisco
Janet H. Johnson, Woodside, CA
Patricia Pearson, Escanaba, MI
Dorothy Scheer, Littleton, CO
Anne McKay, Brooklyn, NY
Dena Goodman, Mill Valley, CA
Sara Slavin, San Francisco
Faye Egan, Fleischmann Yeast, East Hanover, NJ
Frances W. Smith, Universal Foods Corporation,
Milwaukee, WI
Vi Saltzman, Stone-Buhr Milling Company,
Bloomington, MN
B.I.A. Cordon Bleu, Belmont, CA
Forrest Jones, San Francisco
Sue Fisher King, San Francisco
Fillamento, San Francisco
Rushcutters, San Francisco
Royal Chelsea Antiques, San Francisco
By Design, San Francisco
Biordi Art Imports, San Francisco
Crate & Barrel, Chicago
D.F. Saunders & Co., New York
Dean & Deluca, New York
Wolfman, Gold & Good Co., New York
Manhattan Ad Hoc Housewares, New York

Additional Photography
Michael Lamotte, back cover
Laurie Black, Academy photography

Food Styling for Back Cover
Amy Nathan

Food Styling at the Academy
Jeff Van Hanswyk

Calligraphy
Chuck Wertman

Copyediting
Antonio Padial

Editorial Assistance
Jackie Kazarian, Sherri Brody

Color Separations
Color Tech Corporation

Front Cover: Classic yeast breads, such as Cinnamon-Raisin Twirl Loaf (page 34) and Cheddar Cheese Bread (page 33), are delicious main-dish accompaniments and coffee-break snacks.

Back Cover:

Upper left: Leeks, carrots, potatoes, onions, garlic, and herbs are just some of the ingredients that go into a rich veal stock. This stock can later be used in a variety of ways for everything from soup to sauces.

Upper right: Two trouts garnished with lemon and parsley are ready to enter the fish poacher, where they will be simmered in white wine and herbs.

Lower left: Four Cornish game hens are arranged artfully on a platter with baby carrots and green beans. Chefs know that the way food is presented is just as important as how it tastes. You can learn to present food with flair at home.

Lower right: Rosettes of whipped cream are piped onto a cake with a pastry bag and an open-star tip. As a finishing touch, they add a professional look that makes this chocolate cake something special.

Title Page: Fresh ingredients and a cook's care go into homemade breads such as Nell Twomey's Irish Raisin Bread (page 33).

C O N T E N T S

Breads

Homespun Honey-Bran Muffins, handsome Honey Granola Bread, and impressive German Walnut Coffee Ring are sources of satisfaction to bakers.

Bread Basics

Bread baking, like the making of wine and cheese, is an inspired tradition filled with pleasant associations. Baking a handsome loaf, a homespun batch of muffins, or an impressive coffee cake satisfies a fundamental urge for nurture and comfort. There is so much misinformation about the baking of bread, however, that satisfaction can give way to trepidation. The tested baking methods given in this book banish fear of failure, whether you are baking a simple loaf of spicy zucchini bread or a creation as complex as a croissant.

INGREDIENTS

Most recipes for bread call for the same few basic ingredients—flour, liquid, a leavening agent, shortening, eggs, sugar or other sweetener, and salt. The nature of the ingredients, their proportion, and the way they are combined make all the difference in the final product.

Flour, of course, is the fundamental component of most breads. Gluten is an elastic protein substance that gives structure to bread. It develops when liquid combines with two of the proteins contained in wheat flour. Beating, stirring, or kneading a batter or dough creates a strong network to hold the air that inflates the finished product and makes it light.

Wheat is classified as hard or soft depending on its protein content. The amount of gluten in different wheat flours has an important effect on their baking quality.

All-purpose flour is a blend of hard and soft flours suitable for all kinds of home baking, from yeast breads to cakes and pastries. In this book, when a recipe calls simply for "flour," use all-purpose flour.

Unbleached all-purpose flour does not undergo the final stage of the milling process. Its creamy color suits it to rustic, free-form loaves.

Self-rising flour is also an all-purpose flour. Most useful for quick breads, it contains salt and a leavening agent. Self-rising flour can also be used to make yeast breads—omit any salt called for in the recipe—although there's no special advantage in doing so.

Bread flour contains more gluten than all-purpose flour, and some bakers prefer it for certain kinds of yeast breads. Milled from hard wheat, bread flour absorbs slightly more liquid, can take more kneading, and produces dough with greater volume than other flours. When substituting bread flour for all-purpose flour, you can expect to use slightly less flour than called for in the recipe.

Cake flour, on the other hand, is made from soft wheat. Use it only in delicate cakes and pastries.

Many breads are made completely or in part with whole-grain flours. *Whole wheat or graham flour* is milled from the whole kernel: endosperm (the central, starchy cells), bran (the kernel's skin), and germ (the seed-containing portion). Used alone, whole wheat flour produces a heavy, compact, dark bread. Because the wheat germ contains some fat, store whole-wheat flour in a cool, dark place to keep it from becoming rancid.

Rye flour is milled from another grain, one with less gluten than wheat. Available in dark, medium, and light forms, rye flour is usually combined with wheat flour for best results.

Soy flour is made from soybeans, a good source of protein. This flour tends to have a strong flavor, however, so it is usually sparingly in breads containing other flours.

The way in which flour is milled affects the texture of the bread made from it. Flour described as *stone-ground* is coarser than flours made by crushing the grain between smooth metal rollers.

Other grains and cereals used to impart texture and flavor include yellow and white cornmeal, whole-bran cereal, rolled oats, and wheat germ. Bulgur wheat—cracked wheat kernels that have been steamed, dried, and degermed—is an ingredient of the Seven-Grain Bread on page 37.

Measure flour (and indeed any dry ingredient) by spooning it lightly into a measuring cup, then leveling off the top with the straight edge of a metal spatula. It's not necessary to sift flour before measuring when you use the recipes in this book.

Most yeast bread and certain quick bread recipes call for a varying amount of flour (3 to 3½ cups, for example). This is because not every flour will absorb the same amount of liquid. The softness or hardness of the wheat from which the flour was milled affects its absorbency, as does the humidity in the air. Add just enough flour to produce the type of batter or dough described in each recipe.

Liquid in some form is present in most breads. Doughs made with *water* generally yield crisper and crustier breads than doughs made with milk.

Milk used in yeast breads is usually heated to destroy any enzymes that might interfere with yeast action or produce undesirable flavors.

Leavening agents include *baking powder, baking soda,* and *yeast.* The first two are used in muffins, biscuits, and other quick breads. When combined with liquid, baking powder produces carbon dioxide gas, as does baking soda when combined with an acid and liquid. The gas stretches the gluten in the batter or dough, causing the bread to rise and become light.

Yeast fermentation also generates carbon dioxide. Yeast are tiny plants that multiply rapidly when they receive the correct amounts of food, moisture, and warmth. A small amount of sugar supports the growth of yeast, but too much sugar slows the rate. For this reason, rich doughs with a high proportion of sugar take longer to rise than leaner ones.

Before you buy envelopes or packages of yeast, check the expiration date on the wrapper. Be sure you buy no more than you'll use before then. Remember to check that the yeast is still good before using it for any recipe. Cake (compressed) yeast is very perishable and should be kept in the refrigerator; active dry yeast need not be refrigerated.

Yeast is sensitive to heat. Too little and it will not multiply; too much and the yeast will die. The optimum temperature varies according to the type of yeast.

Cake yeast is most effective at about 95° F, *active dry yeast* at about 105° F. *Fast-rising active dry yeast* will tolerate a range of temperatures from 90° to 115° F.

Fast-rising active dry yeast, introduced in 1983, can shorten rising times by half. It is most effective when used in fairly lean doughs and when mixed directly with dry ingredients (rather than being dissolved in water), as in the recipe for Quick-Mix Honeyed Wheat Bread on page 35.

From *other ingredients*, such as shortening, eggs, sugar, and salt, breads derive their distinctive textures and flavors. Salt not only flavors bread but also helps to control the rate of fermentation of yeast breads. In very hot weather, you can add extra salt to help keep yeast doughs from rising too quickly.

The ingredients that go into a loaf of bread are simple—flour, other grains and cereals, yeast, eggs, milk, and sugar or honey. But in concert their effect is almost magical.

The batterie de cuisine *for baking bread ranges from the simplest baking sheet or loaf pan to a sleek heavy-duty electric mixer. Breads pictured here include Chocolate Chip-Orange Bread (page 23) in a clay pan, Pizza Niçoise (page 111) on a glass pizza pan, and Brioche (page 94) in a folding French tin pan.*

BREAD-BAKING UTENSILS

Every baker has a cherished piece of equipment exactly suiting his or her habits—perhaps a special pan that shapes a loaf in a distinctive way or a spatula just flexible enough for transferring soft dough from the mixing bowl to a kneading surface. Here are some of the basic tools many bakers use regularly.

A *heavy-duty electric mixer* takes much of the labor out of the labor-intensive task of making bread. A mixer can beat a fairly heavy dough to develop elasticity so that the dough requires less kneading later. A mixer with a dough hook will knead the dough as well.

Many practiced bread makers use the dough hook of their mixer to knead the dough until it is almost ready to set aside to rise, then finish the job with a minute or two of hand-kneading to be sure the dough feels just right.

Many recipes show methods of combining yeast doughs with your *food processor* (see Food Processor White Bread, page 39; Classic Brioche, page 94; and Easy-Mix Pizza Dough, page 108). Check the instructions for your machine to determine its capacity for heavy dough. Placing too much dough in the machine can damage the motor.

There are a great variety of bread-baking pans available. Standard 4½- by 8½-inch or 5- by 9-inch loaf pans and sturdy, flat baking sheets are essential. Inventively shaped pans aren't necessary but add to the fun of baking.

As with frying pans, the heavier the baking pan, the better and more evenly it holds and conducts heat. Dull, dark pans absorb and hold heat better than shiny ones. Nonstick pans are useful, especially for sweet breads; a nonstick surface makes muffin pans much easier to wash.

Glass pans bake breads nicely. Follow the manufacturer's recommendations—it may be necessary to lower the oven temperature by 25° F for best results. Long available in standard loaf shapes, glass baking dishes can now be found for brioche and pizza.

Many good cooks choose clay pans for baking bread, claiming crisper crusts and a hearth-baked quality. Follow the manufacturer's directions carefully. Some clay pans can be soaked in water before baking to release crust-crisping steam in the oven. Handle clay pans with care when they are very hot (some terra cotta will crack when exposed to sudden changes in temperature).

Accurate measuring equipment is a must, including *measuring spoons* and *measuring cups* for both dry ingredients and liquids. Keep a *spatula* at hand to level off dry ingredients and to loosen baked breads from their pans.

Use a *dough thermometer* to test the liquid used in a yeast bread (remember, too much heat kills yeast); with a *frying thermometer* you will know when fat is at the perfect point for frying doughnuts.

A *pastry brush* for applying an egg glaze should be almost fluffy so that it won't tear the fragile surface of an unbaked dough. Specialty cookware stores stock goose-feather brushes for the particularly gentle job of brushing egg over a delicate brioche.

Wire racks are the surface of choice for cooling baked breads. They let air circulate under and around the bread so that steam won't make the crust soggy.

Finally, once it's time to sample your lovely and laboriously created baked triumph, be sure to slice it with a *serrated knife* to achieve perfect slices.

STORING BAKED BREADS

Because you baked the bread yourself, you know every good ingredient that went into it—it has no preservatives to keep it from going stale or spoiling. Ideally breads are devoured as soon as they are cool, but to save some for another day, place it in a plastic bag or wrap it in foil. Refrigeration actually increases the rate at which bread goes stale, but in humid areas refrigeration may be the only way to keep bread from becoming moldy.

Freezing bread shortly after it has cooled is the best way to preserve it in peak condition. Choose a freezer wrapping that is both moistureproof and vaporproof to keep the bread from drying out or absorbing other flavors and odors. The wrapping should be sturdy enough not to tear when freezer packages are shifted. Possibilities include heavy aluminum foil, coated freezer paper, and strong self-sealing plastic bags. Use frozen breads within four to six months of baking.

Do not glaze, ice, or sugar-dust coffee cakes and rolls that you plan to freeze. Wait to add these decorations after thawing and shortly before serving.

Remove frozen breads several hours before (or the night before) you serve them. Let them thaw at room temperature, then serve as is or warm them in the oven.

TIPS FOR SUCCESS WITH YEAST BREADS

After you've kneaded the dough to just the right consistency—it will take on a silken elasticity and almost seem to assume a life of its own—it is time to plump it into a greased bowl and let it rise in a warm place, ideally about 80° F.

Sometimes it's not easy to find just the right kind of cozy environment for bread to rise at an optimum rate. On a warm day, the kitchen counter might be just right. But with indoor temperatures being kept at an energy-saving level nowadays, you may need to seek a warmer spot in winter. Here are some suggestions:

☐ In a gas oven warmed only by the pilot light.

☐ In a warm electric oven (turn it on at the lowest heat setting for 2 to 3 minutes, then turn it off).

☐ In a convection oven with a low-heat setting for drying foods.

☐ Remember that heat rises; a warm cupboard over your refrigerator or range may be a good place for yeast dough to expand.

You can even let dough rise in the refrigerator for several hours or overnight. When it has risen and you are ready to bake, punch the dough down and let it stand until it reaches room temperature before shaping it.

To test dough to determine if it has risen enough, dent it gently with your index finger. If the dent remains, the dough is ready. If the depression fills up and nearly disappears, the dough needs more time.

Muffins, oven-warm and ready for a breakfast—or lunch or supper—treat, typify the appeal of quick breads.

Quick Breads

Warm muffins, fragrant
fruit-and-nut breads,
crisp-crusted biscuits—
all are quick breads, baked with leavenings
other than yeast. Unlike yeast breads,
quick breads can be readied for the oven
in a few minutes and baked right away.
They are delightful additions to
almost any meal—breakfasts, coffee breaks,
brunch, lunch, tea, family suppers,
and even stylish dinners. If you use
self-rising flour when making quick breads,
omit any baking powder (or baking soda)
and salt called for in
the recipe.

MUFFINS

Making muffins is so easy that you almost risk spoiling them by working too hard at the job. Remember that easy does it.

First mix the flour and other dry ingredients. Then in a separate bowl, blend the liquids—egg, milk, and melted butter or oil. Combining the two mixtures is where a gentle touch is needed: Make a well in the flour mixture, add the liquid all at once, then stir *just enough to moisten the dry ingredients.* The batter should remain rough and slightly lumpy.

Spoon the batter into the baking pans carefully, avoiding additional mixing. Bake muffins in pans that have been well greased, coated with a nonstick finish, or lined with paper baking cups.

You can tell if you've used a light enough hand by looking at the tops of the baked muffins. Ideally the crust has an irregular, pebbled look and the shape is gently rounded. Muffins that are smooth and sharply peaked are likely to be tough and full of long, narrow holes as a result of overmixing.

RAISIN MUFFINS

Here is a basic recipe for muffins with a touch of fruit. The variations include a wholesome whole wheat version, one with pockets of strawberry jam, and a moist, spicy carrot muffin for which you need a blender or food processor.

> 2 cups flour
> ¼ cup sugar
> 1 tablespoon baking powder
> ½ teaspoon salt
> ½ cup raisins
> 1 egg
> 1 cup milk
> 3 tablespoons butter or margarine (melted and cooled) or salad oil
> 1 teaspoon grated orange rind (optional)

1. Preheat oven to 400° F. In a large bowl stir together flour, sugar, baking powder, salt, and raisins.

2. In a medium bowl beat egg with milk, melted butter, and orange rind (if used). Add egg mixture to flour mixture, stirring just until dry ingredients are moistened.

3. Fill greased 2½-inch muffin pans about two-thirds full.

4. Bake until well browned (20 to 25 minutes). Serve warm.

Makes 1 dozen muffins.

Whole Wheat Muffins Use 1 cup *each* whole wheat flour and all-purpose flour. Substitute ¼ cup firmly packed brown sugar for granulated sugar.

Strawberry Nugget Muffins Omit raisins and orange rind. To flour mixture add ⅛ teaspoon ground nutmeg. Fill muffin pans one-third full, using half the batter. To each, add about 1 teaspoon strawberry jam (you will need a total of about ⅓ cup). Use remaining batter to fill pans two-thirds full. Bake as for Raisin Muffins.

Carrot Muffins To flour mixture add ½ teaspoon ground cinnamon; substitute ¼ cup *each* raisins and chopped walnuts for the ½ cup raisins. Combine egg and milk in blender or food processor with ¼ cup salad oil (in place of the 3 tablespoons butter, margarine, or oil), orange rind (if used), and 1 medium carrot (coarsely chopped). Whirl or process until carrot is finely chopped. Add carrot mixture to flour mixture and continue as for Raisin Muffins.

This tempting arrangement of muffins, together with some of the ingredients used to make them, illustrates the diversity of the muffin family.

LEMON DROP MUFFINS

A sprinkling of lemon rind and sugar creates a pebbly tart-sweet crust for these golden muffins.

    2   cups flour
    ¼   cup sugar
    1   tablespoon baking powder
    ½   teaspoon salt
    ⅛   teaspoon ground mace
        or nutmeg
    ¼   cup dried currants
    1   egg
    1   cup milk
    3   tablespoons butter or
        margarine (melted and
        cooled) or salad oil
    1   tablespoon each grated lemon
        rind and lemon juice

Lemon Sugar

    2   teaspoons grated lemon rind
    ⅓   cup sugar

1. Preheat oven to 400° F. In a large bowl stir together flour, sugar, baking powder, salt, mace, and currants.

2. In a medium bowl beat egg with milk, melted butter, lemon rind, and lemon juice. Add egg mixture to flour mixture, stirring only until dry ingredients are moistened.

3. Fill well-greased 2½-inch muffin pans about two-thirds full. Sprinkle tops evenly with Lemon Sugar.

4. Bake until well browned (20 to 25 minutes). Serve warm.

Makes 1 dozen muffins.

Lemon Sugar In a small bowl combine lemon rind and sugar. Mix well, crushing lemon rind with a spoon to release oils into sugar.

HONEY BRAN MUFFINS

Bran muffins are a popular and healthful breakfast bread. These honey-flavored ones contain raisins as well. In the oatmeal spice variation the muffins take on the quality of big, cakelike oatmeal cookies; the banana version has a fruity fillip of flavor.

    1   cup whole-bran cereal
    ½   cup each milk and honey
    1   egg
    ¼   cup butter or margarine,
        softened
    ½   cup raisins
    1   cup flour
    2½ teaspoons baking powder
    ¼   teaspoon salt

1. Preheat oven to 400° F. In a medium bowl combine cereal, milk, and honey; let stand until most of the liquid is absorbed (about 10 minutes). Beat in egg and butter, then mix in raisins.

2. In a large bowl combine flour, baking powder, and salt. Add cereal mixture, mixing just until dry ingredients are moistened.

3. Fill greased 2½-inch muffin pans about two-thirds full.

4. Bake until well browned (20 to 25 minutes). Serve warm.

Makes 1 dozen muffins.

Oatmeal Spice Muffins Substitute 1 cup rolled oats for bran cereal. Increase milk to ¾ cup; omit honey. To flour mixture add ⅓ cup light brown sugar, ¾ teaspoon ground cinnamon, ¼ teaspoon ground allspice, and ¼ cup finely chopped walnuts. Prepare and bake as for Honey Bran Muffins.

Banana Bran Muffins Omit honey and raisins. Combine bran cereal with ½ cup milk and 1 soft ripe medium banana (mashed to a purée). To flour mixture add ⅓ cup *each* sugar and finely chopped walnuts. Prepare as for Honey Bran Muffins. Bake for 25 to 30 minutes.

REFRIGERATOR BRAN MUFFIN MIX

It isn't always convenient to pop into the kitchen at the break of a day and stir up a fresh batch of muffins. But with a container of Refrigerator Bran Muffin Mix at the ready, it isn't necessary—you can spoon out the batter and bake one or two (or more) flavorful and nourishing muffins at a time. The batter can be stored in a tightly covered 6- to 8-cup container for up to two weeks.

    3   cups whole-bran cereal
    1   cup boiling water
    1½ cups all-purpose flour
    1   cup whole wheat or
        graham flour
    2½ teaspoons baking soda
    ½   teaspoon salt
    1   cup raisins
    2   eggs
    1⅓ cups buttermilk
    ½   cup salad oil
    2   teaspoons grated orange rind
    ½   cup each honey and light
        molasses

1. Place cereal in a large bowl; pour boiling water over cereal, stirring to moisten evenly. Set aside until cool (about 10 minutes).

2. Meanwhile, in a very large bowl stir together flours, baking soda, salt, and raisins.

3. Beat eggs into cereal mixture. Blend in buttermilk, oil, orange rind, honey, and molasses. Add cereal mixture to flour mixture, stirring just until dry ingredients are moistened. Bake muffins at once, or store in refrigerator for up to 2 weeks.

4. *To bake muffins:* Preheat oven to 425° F. Spoon batter into greased 2½-inch muffin pans, filling about two-thirds full.

5. Bake until muffins are well browned and spring back when touched lightly (18 to 20 minutes). Serve warm.

Makes 2 to 2½ dozen muffins.

BLUEBERRY CRUMB MUFFINS

Topped with a spiced streusel, these berry muffins are like individual coffee cakes. It's hard to stop at just one.

    2 cups flour
    ¼ cup sugar
    1 tablespoon baking powder
    ½ teaspoon salt
    ¼ teaspoon ground nutmeg
    1 egg
    1 cup milk
    3 tablespoons butter or
      margarine (melted and
      cooled) or salad oil
    1 cup blueberries

Butter Crumb Topping

    ⅓ cup each flour and sugar
    ¼ teaspoon ground cinnamon
    ¼ cup cold butter or margarine

1. Preheat oven to 400° F. In a large bowl stir together flour, sugar, baking powder, salt, and nutmeg.

2. In a medium bowl beat egg with milk and melted butter. Add egg mixture to flour mixture, stirring just until dry ingredients are moistened. Stir in blueberries with last few strokes.

3. Fill greased 2½-inch muffin pans about three-fourths full. Sprinkle tops evenly with Butter Crumb Topping.

4. Bake until well browned (25 to 30 minutes). Serve warm.

Makes 1 dozen muffins.

Butter Crumb Topping In a small bowl mix flour, sugar, and cinnamon. Cut in butter until coarse crumbs form.

OLD-FASHIONED BUTTERMILK CORN STICKS

Corn sticks—and corn muffins and corn bread—are made using the same technique as muffins. They are a flavorful accompaniment to salads, chowders and soups, casseroles, and other savory dishes.

    1 cup each yellow cornmeal
      and flour
    ¼ cup sugar
    2 teaspoons baking powder
    ¾ teaspoon salt
    ½ teaspoon baking soda
    1 egg
    1 cup buttermilk
    2 tablespoons salad oil

1. Preheat oven to 425° F. In a large bowl stir together cornmeal, flour, sugar, baking powder, salt, and baking soda.

2. In a medium bowl beat egg with buttermilk and oil. Add egg mixture to cornmeal mixture and mix just until dry ingredients are moistened.

3. Divide batter evenly into 2 well-greased corn stick pans (or greased 2½-inch muffin pans).

4. Bake until golden brown (15 to 20 minutes). Serve warm.

Makes 14 to 16 corn sticks, or 1 dozen muffins.

CORN BREAD PICANTE

Cheese and green chiles enliven this corn bread from the Southwest. It's good with chili or barbecued ribs.

    1 cup each yellow cornmeal
      and flour
    2 tablespoons sugar
    1 tablespoon baking powder
    ¼ teaspoon salt
    ½ cup shredded Cheddar or
      jack cheese
    2 tablespoons lard or vegetable
      shortening
    1 small onion, finely chopped
    ¼ teaspoon ground cumin
    2 tablespoons butter or
      margarine
    1 can (4 oz) diced green chiles
    1 egg
    1 cup milk

1. Preheat oven to 425° F. In a large bowl stir together cornmeal, flour, sugar, baking powder, and salt until well combined; mix in cheese.

2. Heat lard in a medium frying pan over moderate heat. Add onion and cook, stirring occasionally, until soft and lightly browned. Stir in cumin, then add butter and stir until it melts. Mix in chiles and remove mixture from heat.

3. In a medium bowl beat egg with milk. Stir in onion mixture. Add egg mixture to cornmeal mixture and stir just until dry ingredients are moistened. Spread in a greased 8-inch-square pan.

4. Bake until top browns lightly and a wooden skewer inserted in center comes out clean (20 to 25 minutes). Cut into squares and serve warm.

Serves 6 to 8.

QUICK COFFEE CAKES

Many of these coffee cakes are as simple and speedy to stir together as a batch of muffins, and they're made using exactly the same method for the batter. By varying the kind of baking pan and adding different toppings, you can make them seem quite special.

There are also recipes here for coffee cakes made from a richer, more cakelike batter. For these, butter is creamed with sugar and beaten with eggs before the dry ingredients and liquid are added. Such coffee cakes are delicate enough to serve as desserts, although they are also delicious for a holiday breakfast or weekend brunch, morning coffee, or afternoon tea.

STRAWBERRY RIPPLE TEA CAKE

A cinnamon-spiced streusel crowns this easy yet elegant coffee cake. Bake it in a springform pan so you can present it dramatically.

  1½ cups flour
  ⅓ cup sugar
  2 teaspoons baking powder
  ½ teaspoon salt
  ¼ teaspoon ground nutmeg
  1 egg
  ⅔ cup milk
  ¼ cup butter or margarine (melted and cooled) or salad oil
  ½ cup strawberry jam

Cinnamon Streusel Topping

  ¼ cup flour
  ⅓ cup sugar
  ½ teaspoon ground cinnamon
  3 tablespoons cold butter or margarine

1. Preheat oven to 375° F. In a large bowl stir together flour, sugar, baking powder, salt, and nutmeg.

2. In a medium bowl beat egg with milk and melted butter. Add egg mixture to flour mixture, stirring until mixture is smooth.

3. Spread batter in a greased 8-inch springform pan. Spoon jam evenly over batter. Draw a knife through batter in several back-and-forth strokes to marble jam through it. Sprinkle evenly with Cinnamon Streusel Topping.

4. Bake until topping is well browned and wooden skewer inserted in center comes out clean (40 to 45 minutes).

5. Let stand about 5 minutes, then remove pan sides, cut into wedges, and serve warm or at room temperature.

Serves 6 to 8.

Cinnamon Streusel Topping In a small bowl mix flour, sugar, and cinnamon. Cut in butter until coarse crumbs form.

APRICOT-GLAZED COFFEE RING

Sliced almonds and apricot preserves give this quick coffee cake a shimmering baked-on glaze.

  2 tablespoons butter or margarine, softened
  ½ cup apricot preserves
  ¼ cup sliced almonds
  2 cups flour
  ¾ cup sugar
  2 teaspoons baking powder
  ½ teaspoon salt
  ⅛ teaspoon ground nutmeg
  1 egg
  1 cup milk
  ¼ cup butter or margarine (melted and cooled) or salad oil

1. Preheat oven to 350° F. Coat inside of a 6-cup fluted tube pan with the 2 tablespoons butter. Reserving 2 tablespoons preserves, spoon remaining 6 tablespoons over bottom of pan. Sprinkle with almonds.

2. In a large bowl mix flour, sugar, baking powder, salt, and nutmeg.

3. In a medium bowl beat egg with milk and melted butter. Add egg mixture to flour mixture, stirring until mixture is smooth.

4. Spoon batter lightly into prepared pan. Drizzle reserved 2 tablespoons preserves over top.

5. Bake until top is golden brown and a wooden skewer inserted in thickest part comes out clean (55 minutes to 1 hour).

6. Let stand for a few minutes, then invert onto a serving plate and serve warm.

Serves 6 to 8.

COCONUT-DATE COFFEE CAKE

For a winter brunch, bake this date-studded cake to accompany sliced oranges, omelets filled with ham and shredded Swiss cheese, and coffee.

  1½ cups flour
  ½ cup sugar
  2 teaspoons baking powder
  ½ teaspoon salt
  ½ cup chopped dates
  1 egg
  ¾ cup milk
  ¼ cup butter or margarine (melted and cooled) or salad oil

Coconut Topping

  2 tablespoons flour
  ⅓ cup firmly packed brown sugar
  ½ teaspoon ground cinnamon
  2 tablespoons butter or margarine
  ½ cup flaked coconut

1. Preheat oven to 400° F. In a large bowl stir together flour, sugar, baking powder, salt, and dates.

2. In a medium bowl beat egg with milk and melted butter. Add egg mixture to flour mixture, stirring until mixture is smooth.

3. Spread batter in a greased 8-inch-square pan. Sprinkle Coconut Topping evenly over batter.

4. Bake until topping is golden brown and a wooden skewer inserted in center comes out clean (25 to 30 minutes).

5. Cut into squares and serve warm or at room temperature.

Serves 6.

Coconut Topping In a small bowl stir together flour, brown sugar, and cinnamon. Melt butter; blend with flour mixture. Stir in coconut.

SPICED ALMOND COFFEE CAKE

Cakelike in texture and with the nutty flavor of whole wheat flour, this generously proportioned coffee cake makes a brunch treat to serve a crowd.

> 1½ cups all-purpose flour
> ½ cup whole wheat flour
> 1 teaspoon each *baking powder, baking soda, and ground cinnamon*
> ¼ teaspoon each *salt, ground nutmeg, and ground allspice*
> ½ cup butter or margarine, softened
> 1 cup sugar
> ¾ teaspoon vanilla extract
> 3 eggs
> 1 cup sour cream

Almond Topping

> ½ cup firmly packed brown sugar
> 2 tablespoons flour
> 2 teaspoons ground cinnamon
> 2 tablespoons butter or margarine
> ½ cup sliced almonds

1. Preheat oven to 350° F. Stir together flours, baking powder, baking soda, cinnamon, salt, nutmeg, and allspice.

2. In large bowl of electric mixer, cream butter with sugar until light and fluffy. Blend in vanilla. Then add eggs, one at a time, beating well after each addition.

3. Add flour mixture to creamed mixture alternately with sour cream, mixing to blend after each addition.

4. Spread batter in greased 9- by 13-inch baking pan. Sprinkle evenly with Almond Topping.

5. Bake until almonds are brown and coffee cake tests done when a wooden skewer is inserted in center (30 to 35 minutes).

6. Cut in squares and serve warm or at room temperature.

Serves 8 to 10.

Almond Topping In a medium bowl mix brown sugar, flour, and cinnamon. Cut in butter until coarse crumbs form. Stir in almonds.

An irregular mosaic of strawberry jam nestles beneath the spiced streusel topping of inviting Strawberry Ripple Tea Cake (opposite page).

SOUR CREAM–APPLE COFFEE CAKE

Use a fluted kugelhopf pan, if you have one, to bake this handsome lemon-glazed coffee cake layered with tart apples, golden raisins, and walnuts.

- 3 cups flour
- ¾ teaspoon baking soda
- 1 tablespoon baking powder
- ½ teaspoon salt
- ¾ cup butter or margarine, softened
- 1 cup granulated sugar
- ½ cup firmly packed brown sugar
- 1 teaspoon vanilla extract
- 3 eggs
- 1½ cups sour cream
- 2 medium apples, peeled, cored, and shredded
- ½ cup golden raisins
- 2 tablespoons cold butter or margarine, cut in pieces

Cinnamon-Walnut Filling

- ½ cup sugar
- 1½ teaspoons ground cinnamon
- ½ cup finely chopped walnuts

Lemon Glaze

- ¾ cup confectioners' sugar
- 1 teaspoon soft butter or margarine
- 1 tablespoon warm water
- ½ to 1 tablespoon lemon juice

1. Preheat oven to 350° F. Stir together flour, baking soda, baking powder, and salt.

2. In large bowl of electric mixer, cream the ¾ cup butter with granulated and brown sugars until light and fluffy. Blend in vanilla. Then add eggs, one at a time, beating well after each addition.

3. Add flour mixture to creamed mixture alternately with sour cream, mixing to blend after each addition.

4. In a medium bowl, combine all but ¼ cup of the Cinnamon-Walnut Filling with apples and raisins, stirring to coat apples with cinnamon mixture.

5. Spoon reserved ¼ cup Cinnamon-Walnut Filling over bottom of a well-greased, lightly floured 10-inch kugelhopf, bundt, or other tube pan with a capacity of 10 to 12 cups. Spoon in a third of the batter. Sprinkle evenly with half of the apple filling. Dot with 1 tablespoon of the cold butter. Add another third of the batter, the remaining apple filling, and the last tablespoon butter. Cover with remaining third of the batter.

6. Bake until coffee cake tests done when a long skewer is inserted in thickest part (55 minutes to 1 hour and 10 minutes).

7. Let stand in pan on a wire rack for about 10 minutes, then invert and remove pan. Drizzle Lemon Glaze over warm coffee cake.

Serves 8 to 10.

Cinnamon-Walnut Filling In a small bowl mix sugar, cinnamon, and walnuts.

Lemon Glaze Place confectioners' sugar in a small bowl. Add butter, water, and lemon juice, mixing until smooth and creamy.

MINCEMEAT CRUMB COFFEE CAKE

If you have mincemeat left after baking holiday pies, stir it into a quick coffee cake to greet Thanksgiving or Christmas morning.

- 1½ cups flour
- ½ cup sugar
- 2 teaspoons baking powder
- ½ teaspoon salt
- 1 egg
- ½ cup milk
- 3 tablespoons butter or margarine (melted and cooled) or salad oil
- 1 cup prepared mincemeat

Crumb Topping

- 2 tablespoons flour
- ¼ cup sugar
- 1½ teaspoons ground cinnamon
- 2 tablespoons cold butter or margarine

1. Preheat oven to 400° F. In a large bowl stir together flour, sugar, baking powder, and salt.

2. In a medium bowl beat egg with milk and melted butter. Add egg mixture to flour mixture, stirring until mixture is smooth. Fold in mincemeat.

3. Spread batter in a greased 9-inch-diameter round cake pan. Sprinkle Crumb Topping evenly over batter.

4. Bake until a wooden skewer inserted in center comes out clean (25 to 30 minutes).

5. Cut into wedges and serve warm or at room temperature.

Serves 6.

Crumb Topping In a small bowl stir together flour, sugar, and cinnamon. Cut in butter until coarse crumbs form.

*Easy to bake and easy to like:
Fruited Coffee Ring (page
20), Spiced Almond Coffee Cake
(page 17), and Sour Cream-
Apple Coffee Cake (page 18).*

ALMOND FUDGE COFFEE RING

There's no reason chocolate lovers shouldn't enjoy their favorite flavor at breakfast!

- 1½ cups flour
- 2 teaspoons baking powder
- ¼ teaspoon salt
- ½ cup butter or margarine, softened
- ¾ cup sugar
- ½ teaspoon vanilla extract
- 2 eggs
- ⅔ cup milk
- 2 tablespoons cold butter or margarine, cut into pieces

Cocoa Filling

- 2 tablespoons unsweetened cocoa
- ¼ cup sugar
- ⅓ cup slivered almonds

1. Preheat oven to 350° F. Stir together flour, baking powder, and salt.

2. In large bowl of electric mixer, cream the ½ cup butter with sugar until light and fluffy. Blend in vanilla. Then add eggs, one at a time, beating well after each addition.

3. Add flour mixture to creamed mixture alternately with milk, mixing to blend after each addition.

4. Spoon about a third of the batter into a well-greased, lightly floured 6- to 7-cup fluted tube pan. Sprinkle with half of the Cocoa Filling, then dot with 1 tablespoon of the cold butter. Add another third of the batter, remaining Cocoa Filling, and last 1 tablespoon butter. Cover with remaining third of the batter.

5. Bake until golden brown and tests done when a skewer is inserted in thickest part (45 to 50 minutes).

6. Let stand in pan on a wire rack for about 10 minutes, then invert and remove pan. Serve warm or at room temperature.

Serves 6 to 8.

Cocoa Filling In a small bowl blend together cocoa and sugar; mix in almonds.

FRUITED COFFEE RING

Mixed dried fruits make a colorful mosaic in a sugar-dusted, bundt cake.

- 1 package (8 oz) mixed dried fruits (about 1½ cups)
- 2 cups flour
- 2 teaspoons baking powder
- ¼ teaspoon salt
- ¾ cup butter or margarine, softened
- ¾ cup granulated sugar
- 1 teaspoon vanilla extract
- 2 eggs
- ¾ cup milk
- ¼ cup butter or margarine, melted
- Confectioners' sugar

Brown Sugar Mixture

- ⅔ cup firmly packed light brown sugar
- 1 tablespoon flour
- 1 tablespoon ground cinnamon
- ⅓ cup finely chopped walnuts

1. Preheat oven to 350° F. Place dried fruits in a medium bowl and cover with boiling water. Let stand 10 minutes, then drain fruits and pat dry with paper towels. Chop finely.

2. Stir together flour, baking powder, and salt.

3. In large bowl of electric mixer, cream the ¾ cup butter with the ¾ cup granulated sugar until light and fluffy. Blend in vanilla. Then add eggs, one at a time, beating well after each addition.

4. Add flour mixture to creamed mixture alternately with milk, mixing to blend after each addition. Stir in dried fruits.

5. Spoon a third of the batter into a well-greased, lightly floured 9-inch bundt pan or other tube pan with a capacity of 9 to 10 cups. Sprinkle with half of the Brown Sugar Mixture, then with 2 tablespoons of the melted butter. Add another third of the batter, remaining Brown Sugar Mixture and melted butter. Cover with rest of the batter.

6. Bake until coffee cake tests done when a long skewer is inserted (55 to 65 minutes).

7. Let stand in pan on a wire rack for about 15 minutes, then invert and remove pan. Cool, then dust with confectioners' sugar before serving.

Serves 8.

Brown Sugar Mixture In a small bowl combine brown sugar, flour, cinnamon, and walnuts; mix well.

FRUIT-AND-NUT BREADS

Lessons learned in muffin making stand one in good stead when it comes to baking moist, quick loaves studded with fruits and chopped nuts. The method of combining ingredients is exactly the same.

Although the wonderful smells emanating from the oven as these breads bake may tempt you to taste them while they are still warm, flavor definitely improves if, after cooling, you wrap the bread tightly in foil and allow it to stand for at least a day.

BLUEBERRY-ORANGE-PECAN BREAD

Although it is a bread, this fruit-and-nut loaf is so full of sweet, natural fruit flavors you can serve it as you would a pound cake.

        2 cups flour
        2 teaspoons baking powder
        ½ teaspoon salt
        ¼ teaspoon each *baking soda and ground nutmeg*
        ½ cup sugar
        ½ cup chopped pecans
        2 eggs
        ¼ cup milk
        ½ cup orange juice
        2 teaspoons grated orange rind
        ⅓ cup butter or margarine (melted and cooled) or salad oil
        1 cup blueberries

1. Preheat oven to 350° F. In a large bowl stir together flour, baking powder, salt, baking soda, nutmeg, and sugar. Mix in pecans.

2. In a medium bowl beat eggs with milk, orange juice, and orange rind; blend in butter. Add egg mixture to flour mixture, mixing just until dry ingredients are moistened. Gently fold in blueberries.

3. Spread in a greased, lightly floured, 4½- by 8½-inch loaf pan.

4. Bake until loaf is golden brown and a wooden skewer inserted in center comes out clean (55 minutes to 65 minutes).

5. Let cool in pan for 10 minutes, then turn out onto a wire rack to cool completely.

Makes 1 loaf.

Fresh blueberries (or frozen ones from the summer's harvest) create juicy purple pools in every slice of this orange-nut bread.

For an inviting family meal, make Pumpkin Harvest Bread (opposite page) to accompany an autumn supper of baked beans with chunks of garlic sausage.

2. In a medium bowl beat egg with milk and oils. Blend in banana. Add banana mixture to flour mixture, mixing just until dry ingredients are moistened.

3. Spread batter in a greased, lightly floured 4½- by 8½-inch loaf pan.

4. Bake until loaf is well browned and a wooden skewer inserted in center comes out clean (1 hour and 5 minutes to 1 hour and 10 minutes).

5. Let cool in pan on a wire rack for 10 minutes, then turn out onto rack to cool completely.

Makes 1 loaf.

WHOLE WHEAT ZUCCHINI BREAD

This delicious bread with its touch of lemon is one way to use summer's bounty of zucchini.

>   2 *cups all-purpose flour*
>   1 *cup whole wheat flour*
>   1 *teaspoon each baking soda and salt*
>   ½ *teaspoon baking powder*
>   1½ *teaspoons ground cinnamon*
>   ¼ *teaspoon each ground allspice and nutmeg*
>   1 *cup granulated sugar*
>   1 *cup chopped walnuts*
>   3 *eggs*
>   ½ *cup firmly packed brown sugar*
>   1 *cup salad oil*
>   1 *teaspoon each vanilla extract and grated lemon rind*
>   2 *medium zucchini (unpeeled), coarsely shredded (about 2 cups, lightly packed)*

1. Preheat oven to 350° F. In a large bowl stir together flours, baking soda, salt, baking powder, cinnamon, allspice, nutmeg, and granulated sugar. Mix in walnuts.

2. In a medium bowl beat eggs to blend yolks and whites, then beat in brown sugar, oil, vanilla, and lemon rind. Mix zucchini into egg mixture, then combine with flour mixture, stirring just until dry ingredients are moistened.

JANET'S APRICOT-BANANA BREAD

When you slice this banana bread, the chopped apricots inside form a colorful mosaic. It's good with spiced tea.

>   2 *cups flour*
>   1 *teaspoon baking powder*
>   ½ *teaspoon each baking soda and salt*
>   1 *cup sugar*
>   ⅔ *cup chopped dried apricots*
>   ½ *cup chopped walnuts*
>   1 *egg*
>   ½ *cup milk*
>   2 *tablespoons each walnut oil and salad oil*
>   1 *large, soft ripe banana, mashed (about ¾ cup)*

1. Preheat oven to 350° F. In a large bowl stir together flour, baking powder, baking soda, salt, and sugar. Mix in apricots and walnuts.

3. Divide batter evenly into two greased, lightly floured 4½- by 8½-inch loaf pans.

4. Bake until loaves are well browned and a wooden skewer inserted in center comes out clean (50 minutes to 1 hour).

5. Let cool in pans for 10 minutes, then turn out onto wire racks to cool completely.

Makes 2 loaves.

PUMPKIN HARVEST BREAD

Spicy and moist, pumpkin bread makes a fine and somewhat unconventional accompaniment to hearty autumn fare such as bean soup or baked beans.

2 *cups flour*
2 *teaspoons baking powder*
1 *teaspoon ground cinnamon*
½ *teaspoon ground nutmeg*
¼ *teaspoon each salt, baking soda, ground ginger, and ground cloves*
¼ *cup granulated sugar*
½ *cup chopped walnuts*
¼ *cup raisins*
2 *eggs*
½ *cup firmly packed brown sugar*
1 *cup canned pumpkin*
½ *teaspoon vanilla extract*
⅓ *cup butter or margarine (melted and cooled) or salad oil*

1. Preheat oven to 350° F. In a large bowl stir together flour, baking powder, cinnamon, nutmeg, salt, baking soda, ginger, cloves, and granulated sugar. Mix in walnuts and raisins.

2. In a medium bowl beat eggs to blend yolks and whites, then beat in brown sugar, pumpkin, vanilla, and butter. Add pumpkin mixture to flour mixture, mixing just until dry ingredients are moistened.

3. Spread in a greased, lightly floured 4½- by 8½-inch loaf pan.

4. Bake until loaf is well browned and a wooden skewer inserted in center comes out clean (50 to 55 minutes).

5. Let cool in pan for 10 minutes, then turn out onto a wire rack to cool completely.

Makes 1 loaf.

SPICED FRENCH HONEY BREAD

Classic French *pain d'épice* contains no eggs or shortening, but gets its moist richness from honey and cream. If you wish, you can substitute 2½ teaspoons of Chinese five-spice powder for the anise seed, cinnamon, ginger, and cloves.

½ *teaspoon anise seed*
1 *teaspoon each baking soda and ground cinnamon*
½ *teaspoon each ground ginger and cloves*
¼ *teaspoon salt*
3 *cups flour*
2 *tablespoons dried currants*
¼ *cup firmly packed brown sugar*
¾ *cup honey*
⅔ *cup whipping cream*
⅓ *cup milk*
1 *teaspoon grated orange rind*

1. Preheat oven to 325° F. Whirl anise seed in blender or spice grinder until powdery. In a large bowl mix ground anise seed, baking soda, cinnamon, ginger, cloves, salt, flour, currants, and brown sugar.

2. In a small bowl blend honey, cream, milk, and orange rind. Add honey mixture to flour mixture, stirring just until dry ingredients are moistened.

3. Spread in a greased, lightly floured 4½- by 8½-inch loaf pan.

4. Bake until a skewer inserted in center comes out clean (1 hour and 20 minutes to 1 hour and 30 minutes). Let cool in pan 5 minutes, then turn out onto a rack to cool completely. Wrap and let stand for at least 1 day before slicing thinly to serve.

Makes 1 loaf.

CHOCOLATE CHIP–ORANGE BREAD

The combination of chocolate and orange has wide appeal. Here, it enhances a cakelike bread that's good spread with cream cheese.

2 *cups flour*
2 *teaspoons baking powder*
½ *teaspoon salt*
¼ *teaspoon baking soda*
½ *cup sugar*
½ *cup chopped walnuts*
1 *package (6 oz) semisweet chocolate chips*
2 *eggs*
¼ *cup milk*
½ *cup orange juice*
2 *teaspoons grated orange rind*
1 *teaspoon vanilla extract*
⅓ *cup butter or margarine (melted and cooled) or salad oil*

1. Preheat oven to 350° F. In a large bowl stir together flour, baking powder, salt, baking soda, and sugar. Mix in walnuts and ¾ cup of the chocolate chips.

2. In a medium bowl beat eggs with milk, orange juice, orange rind, and vanilla; blend in butter. Add egg mixture to flour mixture, mixing just until dry ingredients are moistened.

3. Spread in a greased, lightly floured 4½- by 8½-inch loaf pan. Sprinkle evenly with remaining chocolate chips.

4. Bake until golden brown and a wooden pick inserted in center comes out clean (55 minutes to 1 hour).

5. Let cool in pan for 10 minutes, then turn out onto a wire rack to cool completely.

Makes 1 loaf.

Then add liquid, mixing lightly with a fork until a soft dough forms. Turn the dough out onto a sparingly floured surface and work it very lightly with your fingertips until the dough has a uniform consistency and can be formed into a ball. Now the dough is ready to be shaped according to the recipe directions. As with muffin batter, biscuit dough needs a light touch. Avoid working it any more than is necessary.

HAM AND CREAM BISCUITS

Enhance a main-dish salad with these flaky, tender biscuits made with whipping cream and dotted with finely chopped ham.

    2 cups flour
    1 tablespoon baking powder
    ½ teaspoon salt
    ½ cup cold butter or margarine
    ½ cup very finely chopped
        baked ham
    ¾ cup whipping cream

1. Preheat oven to 425° F. In a large bowl thoroughly mix flour, baking powder, and salt. Reserving 2 tablespoons of the butter, cut remaining 6 tablespoons butter into flour mixture until coarse crumbs form.

2. Cook ham in the reserved 2 tablespoons butter in a small frying pan over medium heat, stirring occasionally, until lightly browned. Let cool slightly, then mix lightly into flour mixture.

3. Add cream, all at once, mixing gently just until a soft dough forms. Place dough on a floured board or pastry cloth, turning to coat lightly with flour. Knead gently until you can form into a uniform ball.

4. Roll or pat dough until about ½ inch thick. Cut with a floured 2½-inch round cutter. Place on un-greased baking sheet.

5. Bake until biscuits are golden brown (15 to 20 minutes). Serve hot.

Makes 1 dozen biscuits.

Mastery of the basic biscuit-making technique is rewarded with such special breakfast treats as Orange Pull-Apart Coffee Ring (opposite page) and triangular Cinnamon Scones (page 26).

BISCUITS

The preceding quick breads have all been made from a fairly moist batter. Biscuits and their close relatives, Irish soda bread and scones, start instead with a soft dough.

Solid shortening (butter, margarine, or vegetable shortening) is added to the dry ingredients and then cut in. You can do this using a pastry blender, two knives, or a heavy-duty mixer. Work the mixture until the particles of shortening are uniformly the texture of coarse crumbs.

SESAME-CHEESE BISCUIT RING

Cooked onion and Cheddar cheese flavor this circle of savory biscuits, certain to brighten a family supper of meat loaf or pork chops.

> 6 tablespoons butter or margarine
> 1 small onion, finely chopped
> 2 cups flour
> 1 tablespoon baking powder
> ½ teaspoon salt
> 1 cup shredded sharp Cheddar cheese
> ½ to ⅔ cup milk
> 1 tablespoon sesame seed

1. Preheat oven to 450° F. Melt 1 tablespoon of the butter in a small frying pan over medium heat. Add onion and cook, stirring occasionally, until soft but not brown (5 to 8 minutes). Remove from heat.

2. In a large bowl mix flour, baking powder, salt, and ½ cup of the cheese. Cut in ¼ cup (4 tablespoons) of the remaining butter until mixture is the consistency of coarse crumbs.

3. In a small bowl mix together ½ cup of the milk and the cooked onion. Add milk mixture to flour mixture, stirring lightly just until dough clings together. If dough is too dry, add more milk, 1 tablespoon at a time. Turn out on a floured board or pastry cloth and knead lightly into a ball.

4. Roll dough out ½ inch thick. Cut with a floured 2-inch round cutter. Melt remaining tablespoon of butter and brush over tops of biscuits. Arrange biscuits in a circle, overlapping each other by about ¾ inch, on a well-greased baking sheet. Sprinkle evenly with sesame seed, then with remaining cheese.

5. Bake until golden brown (12 to 15 minutes). Serve hot.

Makes 1 ring, 16 small biscuits.

ORANGE PULL-APART COFFEE RING

Tender orange-flavored biscuit dough shaped into walnut-sized balls and layered with brown sugar and pecans makes a quick and wonderfully gooey coffee ring. Serve it for breakfast or to accompany hot spiced cider for an evening snack.

> 6 tablespoons butter or margarine, melted
> ⅔ cup firmly packed brown sugar
> 2 cups flour
> 2 tablespoons granulated sugar
> ½ teaspoon salt
> ¼ teaspoon ground nutmeg
> 2½ teaspoons baking powder
> 1 tablespoon grated orange rind
> ¼ cup vegetable shortening
> 1 egg
> ½ cup milk
> ¼ cup finely chopped pecans

1. Preheat oven to 400° F. Pour about ¼ cup of the butter into an 8-inch (5½-cup) ring mold. Sprinkle with ⅓ cup of the brown sugar; set pan aside.

2. In a large bowl mix flour, granulated sugar, salt, nutmeg, baking powder, and half of the orange rind. Cut in shortening until mixture is the consistency of coarse crumbs.

3. In a small bowl beat egg with milk until blended. Add egg mixture to flour mixture, stirring lightly just until mixture clings together. Turn out on a floured board or pastry cloth, kneading dough into a ball.

4. In a small bowl mix remaining ⅓ cup brown sugar, remaining 1½ teaspoons orange rind, and pecans.

5. Pinch off pieces of dough the size of walnuts, shape each into a ball, and coat with some of the remaining melted butter. Arrange one layer, spaced slightly apart, in prepared ring mold. Sprinkle evenly with pecan mixture. Place remaining balls of dough over first layer. Drizzle with any remaining butter.

6. Bake until golden brown (25 to 30 minutes). Invert ring mold onto a serving plate and let stand for about 30 seconds. Then remove pan and serve coffee ring hot or warm.

Makes 1 coffee cake.

IRISH SODA BREAD

This currant-studded bread is really a giant biscuit. It makes an inviting breakfast when slathered with butter and marmalade—and also goes nicely with a main-dish soup.

> 2¾ cups unbleached all-purpose flour
> ¼ cup wheat germ
> 3 tablespoons sugar
> 1 teaspoon each baking soda and baking powder
> ½ teaspoon salt
> 3 tablespoons cold butter or margarine
> ½ cup dried currants or raisins
> 1¼ cups buttermilk
> 2 teaspoons milk

1. Preheat oven to 375° F. In a large bowl stir together flour, wheat germ, sugar, baking soda, baking powder, and salt. Cut in butter until mixture is the consistency of coarse crumbs. Stir in currants.

2. Add buttermilk and stir only enough to moisten dry ingredients.

3. Turn dough out onto a floured surface and knead lightly until it is smooth enough to shape into a flattened ball about 1½ inches high. Place on a greased baking sheet and brush with the 2 teaspoons milk. With a floured knife cut an X into the top of the loaf (cutting from the center to within about 1 inch of the edge) about ¼ inch deep.

4. Bake until loaf is golden brown (40 to 45 minutes). Test by inserting a wooden skewer in thickest part.

5. Slide loaf onto a wire rack to cool slightly. Cut into thick slices and serve warm or at room temperature.

Makes 1 round loaf.

HOW TO MAKE BISCUITS

Follow these steps to make light, tender biscuits. This dough is for Ham and Cream Biscuits (see page 24).

1. *Using a pastry blender or two knives, cut shortening (in this case butter) into dry ingredients until flour-coated bits resemble coarse crumbs.*

2. *With a fork, lightly stir in liquid until mixture forms a soft dough that is still a little crumbly in texture—don't overmix.*

3. *Light kneading (use a much gentler touch than for yeast bread) transforms the rough dough into one that can be shaped into a ball and rolled out.*

CINNAMON SCONES

These plump, cinnamon-sugared triangles are a complement to tea, whether a sturdy blend at breakfast or a more delicate one in the afternoon.

>   2 cups flour
>   2 teaspoons baking powder
>   ½ teaspoon baking soda
>   ¼ teaspoon salt
>   ½ cup cold butter or margarine
>   1 egg, separated
>   3 tablespoons honey
>   ⅓ cup buttermilk
>   1 teaspoon water
>   2 tablespoons sugar
>   ¼ teaspoon ground cinnamon

1. Preheat oven to 400° F. In a large bowl stir together flour, baking powder, baking soda, and salt. Cut in butter until mixture is the consistency of coarse crumbs.

2. In a small bowl beat egg yolk with honey and buttermilk until blended. Add buttermilk mixture to flour mixture, mixing lightly just until mixture clings together.

3. With floured hands, lightly shape dough into a flattened ball. Roll out on a floured board or pastry cloth to a circle about ½ inch thick and 8½ inches in diameter. Using a floured knife, cut into 8 or 12 equal wedges. Place on a greased or nonstick baking sheet.

4. In a small bowl beat egg white slightly with water. In another bowl blend sugar and cinnamon. Brush scones lightly with egg white, then sprinkle with cinnamon sugar.

5. Bake until golden brown (10 to 12 minutes). Serve warm.

Makes 8 or 12 scones.

OTHER QUICK BREADS

Not all quick breads can be easily classified. Some of those that follow may not truly be breads at all. But all of these are quick to prepare, and you'll serve them as you do breads—with soups, buttered and jellied, or just for irresistible munching.

SESAME-WHEAT FLATBREAD

Individual rounds of crisp, wheaty bread will remind you of crackers, but their flavor is fresher. They are good with soups or dips and cheeses. Stored airtight in a covered container, they stay fresh at room temperature for a week or more.

>   1⅓ cups all-purpose flour
>   ½ cup whole wheat flour
>   3 tablespoons sesame seed
>   1 tablespoon sugar
>   ½ teaspoon baking soda
>   ¼ teaspoon salt
>   ¼ cup cold butter or margarine
>   ½ cup buttermilk

1. Preheat oven to 400° F. In a large bowl stir together flours, sesame seed, sugar, baking soda, and salt. Cut in butter until mixture forms fine crumbs.

2. Stir in buttermilk, mixing until dough holds together. Use your hands to shape dough into a smooth ball.

3. Pinch off pieces of dough and roll each into a 1-inch ball. Roll out each ball on a floured board or pastry cloth to make paper-thin rounds about 5 inches in diameter. Keep work surface and rolling pin floured as you work, and turn dough several times to keep it from sticking.

4. Place rounds slightly apart on ungreased baking sheets. Bake until golden brown (6 to 8 minutes). Cool on wire racks until crisp (3 to 5 minutes).

Makes about 30 thin flatbreads.

PLUMP POPOVERS

Steam forming in this egg-rich batter billows each popover into a hollow puff that is virtually all crust—the better to lavish with butter and jam. You can make the batter ahead. Complete step 1, cover batter, and refrigerate for up to a day. When ready to bake, stir batter well and proceed with step 2.

    1 cup milk
    3 eggs
    1 tablespoon sugar
    2 tablespoons butter or
      margarine (melted and
      cooled) or salad oil
    1 cup flour
    ¼ teaspoon salt

1. In blender or food processor, combine milk, eggs, sugar, butter, flour, and salt. Whirl until smooth and well combined, stopping motor once or twice and using a spatula to mix in flour from sides of container.

2. Preheat oven to 400° F. Generously grease 2½-inch muffin or popover pans or custard cups. Pour batter into pans, filling about half full.

3. Bake until popovers are well browned and firm to the touch (35 to 40 minutes). Avoid opening oven until end of baking time. Serve hot.

Makes 10 to 12 popovers.

CHEESE PUFF RING

Cream puff pastry (leavened, as are popovers, only by the steam formed from the moisture in the dough) makes a luscious cheese-touched bread to serve as an appetizer or as a salad accompaniment. In France, where it is a traditional specialty in the Burgundy region, this bread is known as *gougère*.

    1 cup milk
    ¼ cup butter or margarine
    ½ teaspoon salt
      Pinch each ground nutmeg
      and cayenne pepper

    1 cup flour
    4 eggs
    1 cup shredded Gruyère or
      Swiss cheese

1. Preheat oven to 375° F. In a 2-quart saucepan combine milk and butter. Place over medium heat and cook, stirring occasionally, until butter melts. Add salt, nutmeg, and cayenne.

2. Add flour all at once, stirring until mixture leaves sides of pan and forms a ball (about 2 minutes). Remove pan from heat.

3. Beat in eggs, one at a time, beating after each addition until mixture is smooth and glossy. Stir in ¾ cup of the cheese.

4. Spoon out dough to make eight equal mounds, slightly apart, in the shape of a ring on a greased baking sheet. Sprinkle with remaining ¼ cup cheese.

5. Bake until puffs are well browned and crisp (40 to 45 minutes). Serve hot.

Makes 1 ring, 8 servings.

To enhance the appeal of an apéritif or preprandial glass of wine, bake a crisp and savory Cheese Puff Ring and serve it warm from the oven.

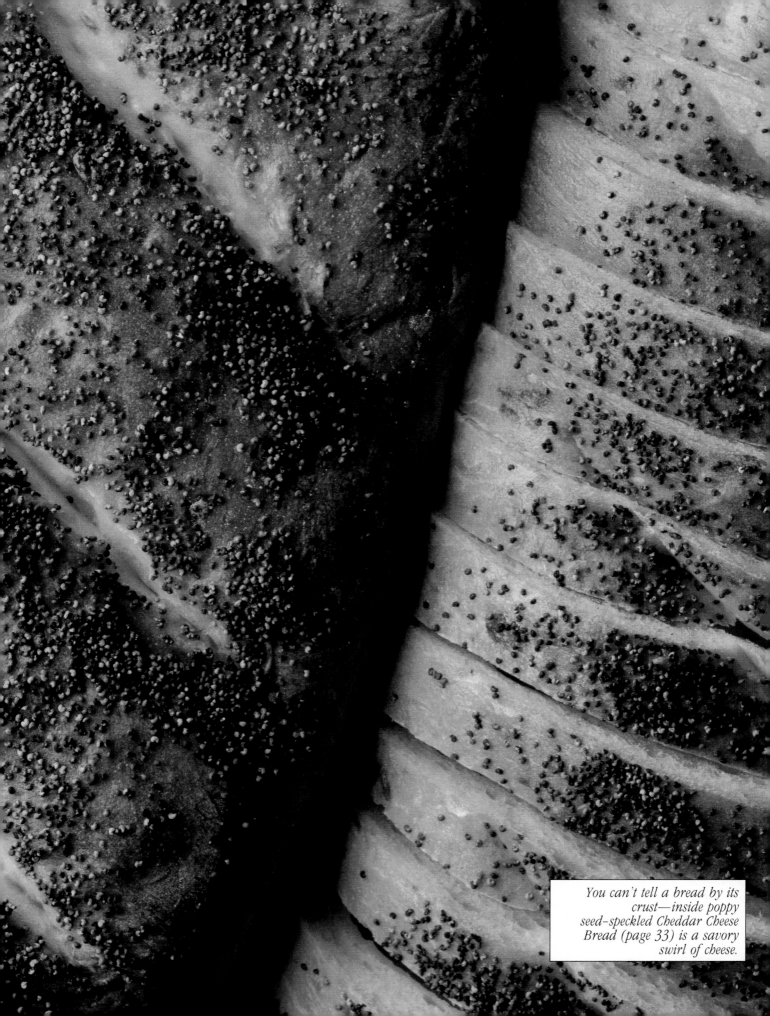

You can't tell a bread by its crust—inside poppy seed-speckled Cheddar Cheese Bread (page 33) is a savory swirl of cheese.

Yeast Breads & Rolls

The world of bread is a temptingly varied one. If you grew up in the United States, the image that comes to mind on hearing the word "bread" is probably that of the standard sliced white loaf that makes peanut butter sandwiches and breakfast toast. To a Frenchman, however, bread (or *pain*) means slender crusty loaves, irresistibly fresh. To a German, the word *Brot* might more readily suggest a dark, fragrant rye bread. One of the joys of baking is recreating some of these splendid loaves to enjoy at home.

HONEST LOAVES

The most basic kinds of yeast breads are baked in deep, rectangular pans. This doesn't mean they must be monotonous. The white breads that follow display a wide range of inventiveness, from the crackly finishing touch of a "Dutch crunch" topping to a swirl of savory cheese inside. Shaping a loaf skillfully adds to its appeal. For tips on a reliable method, see page 36.

Because different ingredients affect browning of breads, every loaf doesn't bake to exactly the same toasty shade of doneness. A good way to determine whether a bread has baked long enough—when color alone doesn't tell you—is to tap it lightly. A hollow sound reassures you that no doughy unbaked spots lurk beneath the crust.

As soon as you decide a loaf of bread is ready to come out of the oven, remove it from the pan onto a wire rack to cool. Wearing oven mitts or using thick potholders, tip the bread out of the pan onto the rack, then turn it right side up. This allows steam to escape, keeps the bread from becoming soggy, and promotes a crust that is crisp on all sides.

On the other hand, you may prefer a soft top crust for certain breads. If so, spread a little butter or margarine over the warm bread.

You may have heard old wives' tales about the ill effects of eating hot bread. While there is probably not much truth in them, it is certain that bread slices better if you allow it to cool to room temperature.

OVERNIGHT WHITE BREAD

Baking yeast bread can be a drawn-out process. These loaves of homey white bread, which rest—shaped and ready to bake—in the refrigerator until the next day, divide the work conveniently.

> 2 packages active dry yeast
> ½ cup warm (105° to 115° F) water
> 2 tablespoons honey
> 1⅔ cups warm (105° to 115° F) milk
> 1½ teaspoons salt
> 2 tablespoons butter or margarine
> 5½ to 6 cups flour
>   Salad oil
> 1 teaspoon butter or margarine, softened (optional)

1. Sprinkle yeast over warm water in large bowl of electric mixer. Add 1 teaspoon of the honey. Let stand until soft (about 5 minutes).

2. Stir in milk, remaining honey, salt, and the 2 tablespoons butter.

3. Add 3 cups of the flour. Blend, then beat at medium speed until smooth and elastic (about 5 minutes). Stir in about 2 cups more flour to make a soft dough.

4. Turn dough out onto a board or pastry cloth dusted with some of the remaining ½ to 1 cup flour. Knead until dough is smooth and satiny and small bubbles form just under surface (10 to 15 minutes), adding just enough flour to prevent dough from being sticky.

5. Cover ball of kneaded dough with plastic wrap and a kitchen towel; let rest for 30 minutes.

6. Punch dough down and divide into two equal portions. Shape each into a loaf (see page 36). Place shaped loaves in greased 4½- by 8½-inch loaf pans. Brush lightly with oil.

7. Cover with plastic wrap and refrigerate for at least 3 hours (up to 24 hours). During this time, dough should nearly double in bulk.

8. Remove from refrigerator and let stand at room temperature for 1 hour.

9. Preheat oven to 375° F. Bake until loaves are well browned and sound hollow when tapped (35 to 40 minutes). Remove loaves from pans and cool on wire racks. If you wish, rub ½ teaspoon of the soft butter over top crust of each loaf while warm.

Makes 2 loaves.

DUTCH CRUNCH LOAVES

A crusty baked-on topping adds distinction to this light, handsome bread. The topping contains sweet rice flour, which is available in Oriental markets.

> 1 package active dry yeast
> 1¼ cups warm (105° to 115° F) water
> 2 tablespoons sugar
> 1 cup warm (105° to 115° F) milk
> 2 tablespoons butter or margarine
> 1½ teaspoons salt
> 6 to 6½ cups flour

Dutch Crunch Topping

> ¼ cup sweet rice flour
> ¼ teaspoon salt
> 1 tablespoon sugar
> 1 tablespoon salad oil
> 4 teaspoons water

1. In large bowl of electric mixer, sprinkle yeast over ¼ cup of the warm water. Add 1 teaspoon of the sugar. Let stand until soft (about 5 minutes).

2. Stir in remaining 1 cup warm water, warm milk, butter, salt, and remaining sugar.

3. Add 4 cups of the flour. Blend, then beat at medium speed until smooth and elastic (about 5 minutes). Stir in about 1½ cups more flour to make a soft dough.

4. Turn dough out onto a board or pastry cloth coated with some of the remaining ½ to 1 cup flour. Knead until dough is smooth and satiny and small bubbles form just under surface (10 to 15 minutes), adding just enough flour to prevent dough from being sticky.

5. Turn dough in a greased bowl. Cover with plastic wrap and a towel; let rise in a warm place until doubled in bulk (1 to 1¼ hours).

6. Punch risen dough down and divide into two equal portions. Shape each into a loaf (see page 36).

Place shaped loaves in greased 4½- by 8½-inch pans.

7. Spread half of the Dutch Crunch Topping evenly over each loaf. Let rise until almost doubled in bulk (45 minutes to 1 hour).

8. Preheat oven to 375° F. Bake until loaves are well browned and sound hollow when tapped (40 to 45 minutes). Remove loaves from pans and cool on wire racks.

Makes 2 loaves.

Dutch Crunch Topping In a small bowl stir together rice flour, salt, and sugar. Blend in oil, then water.

A baked-on topping gives Dutch Crunch Loaves (opposite page) a sweet crispness. It's the center of attraction of this Dutch-style lunch or supper buffet called a koffietafel. *Present the makings for open-face sandwiches, herring, potato salad, and coffee.*

Flour-dusted Potato Bread is a home-style classic, the loaves moist with the goodness of freshly cooked, mashed potatoes.

POTATO BREAD

Mashed fresh potato—and some of the water it cooked in—is the secret of the appealingly moist texture of these classic loaves.

> 1 medium-sized baking potato (6 to 8 oz), peeled and coarsely chopped
> 2 tablespoons butter or margarine
> 2 tablespoons sugar
> 1 teaspoon salt
> 1 cup milk
> 1 package active dry yeast
> 5 to 5½ cups unbleached all-purpose flour

1. Cook potato in a medium saucepan in boiling water to cover until very tender (15 to 20 minutes).

Drain, reserving ¾ cup of the cooking liquid. Pour reserved liquid into large bowl of electric mixer. Cool until just warm to touch (105° to 115° F).

2. Meanwhile, to drained, cooked potato add butter, sugar, and salt. Add 1 to 2 tablespoons of the milk, beating with electric mixer or potato masher until smoothly puréed. Then blend in remaining milk.

3. Sprinkle yeast over warm water in mixer bowl. Let stand until soft (about 5 minutes).

4. Stir in potato mixture. Add 3 cups of the flour. Mix to blend, then beat at medium speed until smooth and elastic (about 5 minutes). Stir in about 1½ cups more flour to make a soft dough.

5. Turn dough out onto a board or pastry cloth coated with some of the remaining ½ to 1 cup flour. Knead until dough is smooth and satiny and small bubbles form just under surface (8 to 10 minutes), adding just enough flour to prevent dough from being sticky.

6. Turn dough in a greased bowl. Cover with plastic wrap and a towel; let rise in a warm place until doubled in bulk (about 1 hour).

7. Punch dough down and divide into two equal portions. Shape each into a loaf. Place shaped loaves in greased 4½- by 8½-inch pans. Dust lightly with a little of the remaining flour. Let rise until almost doubled in bulk (about 45 minutes).

8. Preheat oven to 375° F. Bake until loaves are well browned and sound hollow when tapped (35 to 40 minutes). Remove loaves from pans and let cool on wire racks.

Makes 2 loaves.

CHEDDAR CHEESE BREAD

Nippy cheese swirls through every slice of these golden loaves. The bread is a delicious accompaniment to main-dish salads.

> 1 *package active dry yeast*
> 1¼ *cups warm (105° to 115° F) water*
> 2 *tablespoons sugar*
> 1 *cup warm (105° to 115° F) milk*
> 4 *tablespoons butter or margarine*
> 1 *teaspoon salt*
> 6 *to 6½ cups flour*
> 3 *cups (12 oz) shredded sharp Cheddar cheese*
> 1 *egg white, blended with 1 teaspoon water*
> 2 *teaspoons poppy seed*

1. Sprinkle yeast over ¼ cup of the water in large bowl of electric mixer. Add 1 teaspoon of the sugar. Let stand until soft (about 5 minutes).

2. Stir in remaining water, milk, 2 tablespoons of the butter, salt, and remaining sugar.

3. Add 4 cups of the flour. Mix to blend, then beat at medium speed until smooth and elastic (about 5 minutes). Stir in 1 cup of the cheese, then about 1½ cups more flour to make a soft dough.

4. Turn dough out onto a board or pastry cloth coated with some of the remaining ½ to 1 cup flour. Knead until dough is smooth and satiny and small bubbles form just under surface (12 to 15 minutes), adding just enough more flour to prevent dough from being sticky.

5. Turn dough in a greased bowl. Cover with plastic wrap and a towel; let rise in a warm place until doubled in bulk (1 to 1¼ hours).

6. Punch dough down and divide into two equal portions. Melt remaining 2 tablespoons butter.

7. Roll half of the dough out to a rectangle 8½ inches wide and 14 inches long. Brush lightly with 1 tablespoon of the melted butter, leaving about a ½-inch margin on all edges. Sprinkle 1 cup of the remaining cheese over buttered surface.

8. Starting with an 8½-inch edge, roll dough tightly, jelly-roll fashion. Place in a greased 4½- by 8½-inch loaf pan. Repeat with remaining dough, butter, and cheese. Let loaves rise until almost doubled in bulk (45 minutes to 1 hour).

9. Brush each loaf with egg white mixture, then sprinkle with 1 teaspoon of the poppy seed. Using a razor blade, make three diagonal slashes, about ½ inch deep, in top of each loaf.

10. Preheat oven to 375° F. Bake until loaves are well browned and sound hollow when tapped (35 to 40 minutes). Remove loaves from pans and let cool on wire racks.

Makes 2 loaves.

NELL TWOMEY'S IRISH RAISIN BREAD

This rich, yet light, bread comes from a San Franciscan renowned for her traditional Irish breads.

> 2 *packages active dry yeast*
> 1¼ *cups warm (105° to 115° F) water*
> ½ *cup sugar*
> 1 *cup warm (105° to 115° F) milk*
> ¾ *teaspoon salt*
> ½ *cup butter or margarine, softened*
> 6 *to 6½ cups flour*
> 2 *eggs*
> 2 *cups raisins*

1. Sprinkle yeast over ½ cup of the water in a large bowl of electric mixer. Add 1 teaspoon of the sugar. Let stand until soft (about 5 minutes).

2. Add remaining ¾ cup water, milk, remaining sugar, salt, and butter.

3. Add 3½ cups of flour. Mix to blend, then beat until smooth and elastic (about 5 minutes). Beat in eggs, one at a time, beating well after each addition.

4. Stir in about 2 cups more flour to make a soft dough. Mix in raisins.

5. Turn dough out on a floured board or pastry cloth. Knead until dough is smooth and satiny and small bubbles form just under surface (15 to 20 minutes), adding just enough flour to prevent dough from sticking.

6. Turn dough in a greased bowl. Cover with plastic wrap and a towel; let rise in a warm place until doubled in bulk (1 to 1½ hours).

7. Punch dough down and divide into two equal portions. Shape each into a loaf. Place shaped loaves in greased 5- by 9-inch pans. Let rise until dough just reaches tops of pans (30 to 45 minutes).

8. Preheat oven to 350° F. Bake until loaves are well browned and sound hollow when tapped (35 to 40 minutes). Remove loaves from pans and let cool on wire racks.

Makes 2 loaves.

Apple Wheat Bread (opposite page) makes good lunchbox sandwiches because it's pleasingly moist with shredded tart apple.

CINNAMON-RAISIN TWIRL LOAF

Here is a big, sweetly spiced loaf that bakes to such splendor you may want to serve it as a coffee cake.

> 1 package active dry yeast
> ¼ cup warm (105° to 115° F) water
> ¼ cup sugar
> ½ cup warm (105° to 115° F) milk
> ½ teaspoon each *salt, vanilla extract, and grated orange rind*
> ¼ cup butter or margarine
> 3 to 3¼ cups flour
> 2 eggs
> ½ cup raisins
>   Confectioners' sugar

Cinnamon Sugar

> ⅓ cup sugar
> 1½ teaspoons ground cinnamon

1. Sprinkle yeast over the water in large bowl of electric mixer. Add 1 teaspoon of the sugar. Let stand until soft (about 5 minutes).

2. Add milk, remaining sugar, salt, vanilla, orange rind, and 2 tablespoons of the butter.

3. Add 1½ cups of the flour. Mix to blend, then beat at medium speed until smooth and elastic (about 5 minutes). Beat in eggs, one at a time. Stir in about 1¼ cups more flour to make a soft dough.

4. Turn dough out onto a floured board or pastry cloth. Knead until dough is smooth and satiny and small bubbles form just under surface (10 to 12 minutes), adding just enough flour to prevent dough from being sticky.

5. Turn dough in a greased bowl. Cover with plastic wrap and a towel; let rise in a warm place until doubled (1¼ to 1½ hours). Punch dough down and pat into a ½-inch-thick round on floured surface.

6. Sprinkle raisins over dough. Knead and fold lightly into dough, then shape it into a ball. Roll out to a rectangle 9 inches wide and 18 inches long. Melt remaining 2 tablespoons butter and brush lightly over dough, leaving about a ½-inch margin on all edges. Sprinkle with Cinnamon Sugar.

7. Starting with a 9-inch edge, roll dough tightly, jelly-roll fashion. Pinch edge to seal. Place in a greased 5- by 9-inch loaf pan. Let rise until almost doubled in bulk (45 minutes to 1 hour).

8. Preheat oven to 375° F. Bake until loaf is browned and sounds hollow when tapped (30 to 35 minutes). Remove loaf from pan and let cool on wire rack. While warm, sprinkle lightly with confectioners' sugar.

Makes 1 loaf.

Cinnamon Sugar In a small bowl combine sugar and cinnamon.

WHOLESOME WHOLE-GRAIN LOAVES

Whole-grain flours add another dimension of flavor, as well as texture, to baking. Their variety—both in grains and in different forms of the same cereal—is extensive (see flour descriptions on page 6).

When you bake breads with whole-grain flours, you're on sound nutritional ground because they abound in both the complex carbohydrates and the natural fiber nutrition experts recommend to improve overall diet.

In the recipes that follow (and those beginning on page 44), you'll note that whole-grain flours are not the only kind used. A yeast bread made with only whole wheat flour, for example, is considerably denser and heavier than the same size loaf made from all-purpose flour. Mixing all-purpose flour with whole wheat or other whole-grain flours produces bread of greater volume and lighter texture.

QUICK-MIX HONEYED WHEAT BREAD

Using fast-rising active dry yeast, you can produce a light, fine-textured whole wheat bread that is faster to make than most yeast breads for several reasons. You mix the yeast with the other dry ingredients without first softening it in hot water; the dough needs only one rising—after it is shaped into loaves—and it rises faster than most whole-grain breads.

5¼ to 5¾ cups all-purpose flour
2 cups whole wheat flour
2 packages fast-rising active dry yeast
2 teaspoons salt
2 cups milk
½ cup water
½ cup honey
2 tablespoons salad oil

1. In large bowl of electric mixer combine 4 cups of the all-purpose flour, the whole wheat flour, yeast, and salt; stir to blend dry ingredients thoroughly.

2. In a 1½- to 2-quart saucepan combine milk, water, honey, and oil; place over medium heat, stirring to blend well, until hot to touch (110° to 115° F).

3. Add milk mixture to flour mixture. Mix to blend, then beat at medium speed until smooth and elastic (about 5 minutes). Stir in about ¾ cup of the remaining all-purpose flour to make a soft dough.

4. Turn dough out onto a board or pastry cloth coated with some of the remaining ½ to 1 cup flour. Knead until dough is smooth and satiny and small bubbles form just under surface (about 10 minutes), adding just enough flour to prevent dough from being sticky.

5. Cover dough and let rest for 10 minutes.

6. Divide dough into two equal portions. Shape each into a loaf. Place shaped loaves in greased 4½- by 8½-inch loaf pans. Cover lightly with waxed paper or plastic wrap. Let rise in a warm place until doubled in bulk (40 to 45 minutes).

7. Preheat oven to 375° F. Bake until loaves are well browned and sound hollow when tapped (30 to 45 minutes). Remove loaves from pans and let cool on wire racks.

Makes 2 loaves.

APPLE WHEAT BREAD

Shredded apple in this mild, wheaty bread adds an elusive flavor and keeps it moist.

1 package active dry yeast
1¼ cups warm (105° to 115° F) water
¼ cup firmly packed brown sugar
1 cup warm (105° to 115° F) milk
1½ teaspoons salt
2 tablespoons salad oil
4¾ to 5¼ cups unbleached all-purpose flour
1½ cups whole wheat or graham flour
1 large apple, peeled, cored, and shredded

1. Sprinkle yeast over ¼ cup of the water in large bowl of electric mixer. Add 1 teaspoon of the brown sugar. Let stand until soft (about 5 minutes).

2. Stir in remaining water, milk, remaining brown sugar, salt, and oil.

3. Add 3½ cups of the unbleached flour. Mix to blend, then beat at medium speed until smooth and elastic (about 5 minutes). Stir in whole wheat flour and apple. Then stir in about ¾ cup more unbleached flour to make a soft dough.

4. Turn dough out onto a board or pastry cloth coated with some of the remaining ½ to 1 cup unbleached flour. Knead until dough is smooth and springy and small bubbles form just under surface (12 to 15 minutes), adding just enough flour to prevent dough from being sticky.

5. Turn dough in a greased bowl. Cover with plastic wrap and a towel; let rise in a warm place until doubled in bulk (1¼ to 1½ hours).

6. Punch dough down and divide into two equal portions. Shape each into a loaf. Place loaves in greased 4½- by 8½-inch loaf pans. Let rise until almost doubled in bulk (40 to 45 minutes).

7. Preheat oven to 350° F. Bake until loaves are well browned and sound hollow when tapped (40 to 45 minutes). Remove loaves from pans and let cool on wire racks.

Makes 2 loaves.

HOW TO KNEAD AND SHAPE A LOAF

Transforming a rather amorphous mass into a smooth, bouncy dough that yields a lovely loaf begins with kneading.

1. *Knead gently, using heels of your hands. Increase pressure as dough becomes elastic. Push dough away, then turn it and repeat the rhythmic motion.*

2. *After dough has risen until doubled, punch it down—use your fist in a straight-down motion. Now it is ready to shape into loaves or rolls.*

3. *To shape a standard loaf, pat or roll the dough out to a rectangle the width of the loaf pan and about twice as long as it is wide.*

4. *Beginning with a narrow end, roll the dough tightly as if you were making a jelly roll. A smooth technique will prevent large air pockets.*

5. *Seal edges by pinching firmly (moisten lightly with water if dough seems dry). Place seam side down in greased loaf pan. Bread is ready to bake when rounded edge of dough rises above pan rim. "Oven spring" will increase volume during the first minutes of baking.*

CORNISH BROWN BREAD

This coarse-textured bread with whole wheat or graham flour and a sprinkling of currants boasts a delicious flavor. You might try it with a British farm cheese such as Caerphilly. Treacle (English molasses) gives an authentic touch, but any dark molasses can be used.

    1 package active dry yeast
 1¼ cups warm (105° to 115°F)
      water
   ¼ cup dark treacle or dark
      molasses
    1 cup warm (105° to 115°F)
      milk
 1½ teaspoons salt
    2 tablespoons butter or
      margarine, softened
    4 to 4½ cups unbleached
      all-purpose flour
 2½ cups whole wheat or
      graham flour
   ¼ cup dried currants

1. Sprinkle yeast over ¼ cup of the water in large bowl of electric mixer. Add 1 teaspoon of the treacle. Let stand until soft (about 5 minutes).

2. Stir in remaining water, milk, treacle, salt, and butter.

3. Add 3½ cups of the unbleached flour. Mix to blend, then beat at medium speed until smooth and elastic (about 5 minutes). Stir in whole wheat flour to make a soft dough; mix in currants.

4. Turn dough out onto a board or pastry cloth floured with some of the remaining ½ to 1 cup unbleached flour. Knead until dough is smooth and springy and small bubbles form just under surface (12 to 15 minutes), adding just enough more flour to prevent dough from being sticky.

5. Turn dough in a greased bowl. Cover with plastic wrap and a towel; let rise in a warm place until doubled in bulk (about 1½ hours).

6. Punch dough down and divide into two equal portions. Shape each into a loaf (see opposite page). Place shaped loaves in greased 4½- by 8½-inch loaf pans. Let rise until almost doubled in bulk (about 1 hour).

7. Preheat oven to 350° F. Bake until loaves are well browned and sound hollow when tapped (40 to 45 minutes). Remove loaves from pans and let cool on wire racks.

Makes 2 loaves.

NUT-BROWN ALE BREAD

The bottle of dark ale in this bread explains the malty tang of its flavor, and the combination of wheat germ, rye flour, and unbleached flour makes it pleasantly crusty.

> 2 packages active dry yeast
> 1 cup warm (105° to 115° F) water
> ⅓ cup firmly packed brown sugar
> 1 bottle or can (12 oz) dark ale, warmed to 105° to 115° F
> 2 teaspoons salt
> 2 tablespoons butter or margarine
> 1 cup wheat germ
> 5 to 5½ cups unbleached all-purpose flour
> 1 cup medium rye flour

1. Sprinkle yeast over ½ cup of the water in large bowl of electric mixer. Add 1 teaspoon of the brown sugar. Let stand until soft (about 5 minutes).

2. Stir in ale, salt, butter, and remaining water and brown sugar.

3. Add wheat germ and 3½ cups of the unbleached flour. Mix to blend, then beat at medium speed until smooth and elastic (about 5 minutes). Stir in rye flour, then about 1 cup more unbleached flour to make a soft dough.

4. Turn dough out onto a board or pastry cloth floured with some of the remaining ½ to 1 cup unbleached flour. Knead until dough is springy and small bubbles form just under surface (12 to 15 minutes), adding just enough more flour to prevent dough from being sticky.

5. Turn dough in a greased bowl. Cover with plastic wrap and a towel; let rise in a warm place until doubled in bulk (about 1 hour).

6. Punch dough down and divide into two equal portions. Shape each into a loaf (see opposite page). Place shaped loaves in greased 4½- by 8½-inch loaf pans. Let rise until almost doubled in bulk (35 to 45 minutes).

7. Preheat oven to 375° F. Bake until loaves are well browned and sound hollow when tapped (40 to 45 minutes). Remove loaves from pans and let cool on wire racks.

Makes 2 loaves.

SEVEN-GRAIN BREAD

There are seven different kinds of grains in these chewy loaves, and each adds a different flavor note to the background provided by unbleached flour.

> 2 cups warm (105° to 115° F) water
> ½ cup bulgur wheat
> 2 packages active dry yeast
> ¼ cup light molasses
> 1 cup warm (105° to 115° F) milk
> 2 teaspoons salt
> 2 tablespoons salad oil
> 1 cup quick-cooking rolled oats
> 4 to 4½ cups unbleached all-purpose flour
> ¼ cup each soy flour and wheat germ
> ½ cup each medium rye flour and whole wheat or graham flour

1. Bring 1½ cups of the water to a boil; pour over bulgur wheat in a medium bowl. Set aside until mixture cools slightly (about 15 minutes).

2. Pour remaining ½ cup warm water into large bowl of electric mixer. Sprinkle yeast over water. Add 1 teaspoon of the molasses. Let stand until soft (about 5 minutes).

3. Stir in milk, remaining molasses, salt, and oil; blend in cooled bulgur mixture and rolled oats.

4. Add 3 cups of the unbleached flour. Mix to blend, then beat at medium speed until smooth and elastic (about 5 minutes). Stir in soy flour and wheat germ. Then gradually blend in rye and whole wheat flours. Stir in about ½ cup more unbleached flour to make a soft dough.

5. Turn dough out onto a board or pastry cloth coated with some of the remaining ½ to 1 cup unbleached flour. Knead until dough is smooth and springy and small bubbles form just under surface (12 to 15 minutes), adding enough flour to prevent dough from being sticky.

6. Turn dough in a greased bowl. Cover with plastic wrap and a towel; let rise in a warm place until doubled in bulk (1¼ to 1½ hours).

7. Punch dough down and divide into two equal portions. Shape each into a loaf (see opposite page). Place shaped loaves in greased 4½- by 8½-inch pans. Let rise until almost doubled in bulk (30 to 45 minutes).

8. Preheat oven to 350° F. Bake until loaves are well browned and sound hollow when tapped (45 to 50 minutes). Remove loaves from pans and let cool on wire racks.

Makes 2 loaves.

If your mother came from Ireland—or England— she may remember one of these breads. Clockwise from upper left: Nell Twomey's Irish Raisin Bread (page 33), Nut-Brown Ale Bread (page 37), and Cornish Brown Bread (page 36).

HONEY GRANOLA BREAD

Choose your favorite fruit-and-nut granola cereal to enhance this honey-sweetened whole wheat bread.

> 2 *packages active dry yeast*
> 1¼ *cups warm (105° to 115° F) water*
> ⅓ *cup honey*
> 1 *cup warm (105° to 115° F) milk*
> 2 *teaspoons salt*
> 2 *tablespoons salad oil*
> 2 *cups whole wheat flour*
> 4 *to 4½ cups unbleached all-purpose flour*
> 1 *cup granola cereal*

1. Sprinkle yeast over ½ cup of the water in large bowl of electric mixer. Add 1 teaspoon of the honey. Let stand until soft (about 5 minutes).

2. Stir in remaining ¾ cup water, milk, remaining honey, salt, and oil.

3. Add whole wheat flour and 2½ cups of the unbleached flour. Mix to blend; then beat at medium speed until smooth and elastic (about 5 minutes). Stir in granola, then about

1 cup of the unbleached flour to make a soft dough.

4. Turn dough out onto a floured board or pastry cloth. Knead until springy and small bubbles form just under surface (10 to 12 minutes), adding enough of remaining flour to prevent dough from being sticky.

5. Turn dough in a greased bowl. Cover with plastic wrap and a towel; let rise in a warm place until doubled in bulk (about 1 hour).

6. Punch dough down and divide into two equal portions. Shape into loaves (see page 36). Place loaves in greased 4½- by 8½-inch pans. Let rise until almost doubled in bulk (40 to 45 minutes).

7. Preheat oven to 350° F. Bake until loaves are well browned and sound hollow when tapped (40 to 45 minutes). Remove loaves from pans and let cool on wire racks.

Makes 2 loaves.

FOOD PROCESSOR BREAD

Using a food processor can take much of the toil out of baking yeast breads. The processor, fitted with its steel blade, not only mixes the dough but also kneads it—all in mere seconds.

If the dough seems a bit too sticky after you've added all the liquid in step four, add more flour—a tablespoon at a time—until it feels satiny smooth.

Because some smaller processors can only handle a limited amount of flour at a time, this recipe makes a single loaf. But it's so quick to prepare the dough, you'll find yourself baking this delicious bread often.

FOOD PROCESSOR WHITE BREAD

> 1 package active dry yeast
> ¼ cup warm (105° to 115° F) water
> 1 tablespoon honey
> 2¾ to 3 cups flour
> ¾ teaspoon salt
> ⅔ cup warm (105° to 115° F) milk
> 1 tablespoon salad oil

1. Sprinkle yeast over the warm water in a measuring cup. Add honey. Let stand until soft (about 5 minutes).

2. In food processor bowl fitted with steel blade, combine 2¾ cups flour and the salt; whirl to mix.

3. Stir warm milk and oil into yeast mixture.

4. With processor running, pour yeast mixture through feed tube in a steady stream. Adjust the amount poured so flour can absorb it. Process until dough forms a ball.

5. Turn off processor. Dough should feel barely sticky. If too soft, add some of the remaining ¼ cup flour, 1 tablespoon at a time, just until dough feels soft, smooth, and satiny.

6. Knead by processing for an additional 20 seconds.

7. Shape dough into a ball. Turn dough in a greased bowl. Cover with plastic wrap and a towel; let rise in a warm place until doubled in bulk (45 minutes to 1 hour).

8. Punch dough down and shape into a loaf (see page 36). Place shaped loaf in a greased 4½- by 8½-inch loaf pan. Let rise until almost doubled in bulk (30 to 45 minutes).

9. Preheat oven to 375° F. Bake until loaf is well browned and sounds hollow when tapped (35 to 40 minutes). Remove loaf from pan and let cool on a wire rack.

Makes 1 loaf.

FREE-FORM LOAVES

No other dish is as likely to elicit a chorus of oh's and ah's at the table as fragrant, home-baked bread. Perhaps it's because we have all become so accustomed to bakery bread. When the bread has the boutique look that no baking pan can achieve, the exclamations are all the more likely to take on the quality of applause.

Even if you're baking more for personal satisfaction than public acclaim, the breads you shape inventively are especially rewarding. So many possibilities exist—plump spheres, ringlike wreaths, slender baguettes, stubby ovals.

Mixing in either flavorful seasonings or toothsome whole grains and savory seeds adds to the drama of the breads that follow.

SWEET RED PEPPER LOAVES

Chopped sweet red bell pepper, sautéed in olive oil, speckles these little loaves of crusty French bread and tinges them with a golden color. Serving a bread like this with barbecued meat or chicken and a green salad makes a meal that's very special.

    2 tablespoons olive oil
    1 sweet red bell pepper, seeded
      and finely chopped
    1 package active dry yeast
    1⅓ cups warm (105° to 115° F)
      water
    1 tablespoon sugar
    1½ teaspoons salt
    3¾ to 4¼ cups bread flour
    1 teaspoon cornstarch,
      blended with ⅓ cup water

1. Heat oil in a medium frying pan over moderate heat. Add red pepper and cook, stirring often, until soft but not browned (about 5 minutes). Remove from heat and let stand for about 10 minutes to cool.

2. Sprinkle yeast over ⅓ cup of the water in large bowl of electric mixer. Add sugar. Let stand until soft (about 5 minutes).

3. Stir in remaining 1 cup water, red pepper mixture, and salt.

4. Add 2¼ cups of the flour. Mix to blend; then beat at medium speed until smooth and elastic (about 5 minutes). Stir in about 1 cup more flour to make a soft dough.

5. Turn dough out onto a board or pastry cloth coated with some of the remaining ½ to 1 cup flour. Knead until dough is springy and small bubbles form just under surface (20 to 25 minutes), adding just enough more flour to prevent dough from being sticky.

6. Turn dough in a greased bowl. Cover with plastic wrap and a towel; let rise in a warm place until doubled in bulk (about 1 hour).

7. Punch dough down; cover and let rest for 10 minutes. Divide into two equal portions. Shape each into a round ball. Place on greased baking sheets. Let rise until almost doubled in bulk (30 to 45 minutes).

8. Preheat oven to 375° F. Bring cornstarch mixture to a boil in a small pan over medium-high heat, stirring until thick and clear. Brush each loaf with warm cornstarch mixture. With a razor blade cut a large X about ½ inch deep at center of each loaf.

9. Bake until loaves are brown and sound hollow when tapped (30 to 35 minutes). Transfer to wire racks to cool.

Makes 2 small, round loaves.

FRENCH FILBERT OR WALNUT BREAD

In France, the bread that accompanies a postprandial cheese course is often a rustic loaf studded with finely chopped filberts or walnuts. Either is appetizing, but walnuts transform the color of the bread as well as add flavor—the crumb takes on a darker tone similar to that of rye bread.

    2 packages active dry yeast
    2 cups warm (105° to 115° F)
      water
    2 teaspoons sugar
    1½ teaspoons salt
    2 tablespoons butter or
      margarine, softened
    5¼ to 5¾ cups unbleached
      all-purpose flour
    ¾ cup finely chopped filberts
      or walnuts
    1 egg white, slightly beaten
      with 2 teaspoons water

1. Sprinkle yeast over ½ cup of the water in large bowl of electric mixer. Add sugar. Let stand until soft (about 5 minutes).

2. Stir in remaining 1½ cups water, salt, and butter.

3. Add 3½ cups of the flour. Mix to blend; then beat at medium speed until smooth and elastic (about 5 minutes). Stir in filberts, then about 1½ cups more flour to make a soft dough.

4. Turn dough out onto a board or pastry cloth coated with some of the remaining ¼ to ¾ cup flour. Knead until dough is springy and small bubbles form just under surface (20 to 25 minutes), adding just enough more flour to prevent dough from being sticky.

5. Turn dough in a greased bowl. Cover with plastic wrap and a towel; let rise in a warm place until doubled in bulk (about 1 hour).

6. Punch dough down; cover and let rest for 10 minutes. Divide into two equal portions. Shape each into a round ball. Place on greased baking sheets. Let rise until almost doubled in bulk (40 to 45 minutes).

7. Preheat oven to 375° F. Brush loaves lightly with egg white mixture. Sift a little of the flour over that. With a razor blade make two parallel cuts about ½ inch deep in each

direction (forming a tic-tac-toe design) across each loaf.

8. Bake until loaves are brown and sound hollow when tapped (40 to 45 minutes). Transfer to wire racks to cool.

Makes 2 round loaves.

Sweet Red Pepper Loaves (opposite page) taste good with Italian food such as the creamy mostaccioli carbonara shown here, served with white wine and a green salad.

41

Sesame Bread Ring, served with an 8-inch wheel of ripe Brie cheese placed in the middle, makes an inviting centerpiece for a wine-tasting party.

MEXICAN EGG, ANISE, AND SESAME BREAD

Plump rounds of this bread are a feature of the Saturday market in the city of Oaxaca, where they are called *pan de yama.* The bread is wonderful served warm with butter.

> *2 packages active dry yeast*
> *½ cup warm (105° to 115° F) water*
> *½ cup sugar*
> *1 cup warm (105° to 115° F) milk*
> *1½ teaspoons salt*
> *½ teaspoon anise seed, coarsely crushed*
> *¼ cup each butter or margarine and lard, softened*
> *5½ to 5¾ cups flour*
> *3 egg yolks*
> *1 egg white, beaten with 2 teaspoons water*
> *2 teaspoons sesame seed*

1. Sprinkle yeast over the water in large bowl of electric mixer. Add 1 teaspoon of the sugar. Let stand until soft (about 5 minutes). Add milk, remaining sugar, salt, anise seed, butter, and lard. Stir until sugar dissolves.

2. Add 2½ cups of the flour. Blend, then beat at medium speed to make a smooth batter (about 5 minutes). Cover and let stand in a warm place until bubbly (about 20 minutes).

3. Beat in egg yolks, one at a time. Gradually stir in about 2½ cups more flour to make a soft dough.

4. Turn dough out onto a floured board or pastry cloth. Knead until smooth and satiny and small bubbles form just under surface (20 to 25 minutes). Add flour to prevent dough from being too sticky.

5. Turn dough in a greased bowl. Cover and let rise in a warm place until doubled in bulk (1 to 1¼ hours). Punch dough down, turn out on a floured surface, cover with inverted bowl, and let rest for 10 minutes.

6. Divide dough into two equal portions. Shape each portion into a ball. Place on greased baking sheets. Let rise until almost doubled in bulk (30 to 40 minutes).

7. Preheat oven to 375° F. Brush loaves lightly with egg white mixture. Sprinkle evenly with sesame seed. Using a razor blade cut a slash about ½ inch deep across the center, cutting from side to side.

8. Bake until loaves are well browned (25 to 30 minutes). Test with a long wooden skewer. Slide loaves onto wire racks to cool.

Makes 2 round loaves.

SESAME BREAD RING

One way to serve bread with cheese is to bake a ring to encircle a whole cheese. This sesame-sprinkled bread is designed to fit an 8-inch round of Brie (about 2 pounds).

> *1 package active dry yeast*
> *1 cup warm (105° to 115° F) water*
> *1 tablespoon sugar*
> *½ cup warm (105° to 115° F) milk*
> *1 tablespoon olive oil*
> *1 teaspoon salt*
> *4¼ to 4½ cups flour*
> *1 egg, beaten with 2 teaspoons water*
> *2 tablespoons sesame seed*
> *1 whole (about 2 lbs) 8-inch round Brie cheese (optional)*

1. Sprinkle yeast over ¼ cup of the water in large bowl of electric mixer. Add sugar. Let stand until soft (about 5 minutes).

2. Stir in remaining ¾ cup warm water, warm milk, olive oil, and salt.

3. Add 2½ cups of the flour. Mix to blend, then beat at medium speed until smooth and elastic (about 5 minutes). Stir in about 1¼ cups more flour to make a soft dough.

4. Turn dough out onto a board or pastry cloth coated with some of the remaining ½ to ¾ cup flour. Knead until dough is smooth and satiny and small bubbles form just under surface (12 to 15 minutes), adding just enough flour to prevent dough from being sticky.

5. Turn dough in a greased bowl. Cover with plastic wrap and a towel; let rise in a warm place until doubled in bulk (45 minutes to 1 hour).

6. Punch dough down. Shape into a ball, cover with inverted bowl, and let rest 10 minutes. Then flatten to make a circle 1 inch thick. Cut a 1-inch X in center with scissors or a knife. Use your hands to pull dough away from center, smoothing and shaping dough into a ring with a center area 8 inches in diameter.

7. If you wish to serve ring of bread around whole Brie cheese, grease outside of an 8-inch-round cake pan; invert it in center of a large, well-greased baking sheet or pizza pan. Place bread ring on baking sheet (with cake pan in center). Let rise until almost doubled in bulk (30 to 40 minutes).

8. Preheat oven to 425° F. Leaving cake pan in place, lightly brush dough with egg mixture, being careful not to let it collect around cake pan. Sprinkle bread ring with sesame seed.

9. Bake for 5 minutes. Reduce heat to 350° F and continue baking until bread is well browned and sounds hollow when tapped (20 to 25 minutes). Use a spatula to loosen bread around cake pan. Carefully lift bread ring up and transfer to a wire rack to cool.

10. Serve bread with Brie in center; cut several slices from ring to spread it enough to make room for the cheese. Slice remaining bread as needed to accompany cheese.

Makes 1 large (13-inch diameter) ring.

PARMESAN AND PEPPER BREAD

This Italian-style bread has a richness of flavor that makes it a satisfying part of a soup or salad supper.

   1 *package active dry yeast*
1½ *cups warm (105°F to 115°F) water*
   1 *tablespoon sugar*
1½ *teaspoons salt*
  ½ *teaspoon coarsely ground black pepper*
   2 *tablespoons olive oil*
3½ *to 4 cups unbleached all-purpose flour*
  ½ *cup grated Parmesan cheese*
   1 *egg white, blended with 2 teaspoons water*

1. Sprinkle yeast over the water in large bowl of electric mixer. Add sugar. Let stand until yeast is soft (about 5 minutes).

2. Stir in salt, pepper, and oil. Add 2½ cups of the flour. Mix to blend, then beat at medium speed until smooth and elastic (about 5 minutes). Stir in 6 tablespoons of the Parmesan cheese and about 1 cup more flour to make a soft dough.

3. Turn dough out onto a floured board or pastry cloth. Knead until springy and small bubbles form just under surface (15 to 20 minutes), adding just enough flour to prevent dough from being sticky.

4. Turn dough in a greased bowl. Cover with plastic wrap and a towel; let rise in a warm place until doubled in bulk (60 to 75 minutes).

5. Punch dough down; knead dough lightly into a ball. Cover with inverted bowl and let rest for 10 minutes. Divide dough into two equal portions. Shape each into a slender oval loaf about 14 inches long. Place well apart on a large, greased baking sheet. Let rise until almost doubled in bulk (25 to 35 minutes).

6. Preheat oven to 375° F. Brush loaves lightly with egg white mixture. Sprinkle 1 tablespoon cheese over each loaf. With a razor blade make three diagonal slashes, about ½ inch deep, down center of each loaf.

7. Bake until loaves are golden brown and sound hollow when tapped (25 to 30 minutes). Transfer to wire racks to cool.

Makes 2 long loaves.

FRENCH COUNTRY BREAD-IN-A-BASKET

This country bread, or *pain de campagne*, rises in a flour-dusted basket, acquiring an imprint that remains as it bakes.

   1 *package active dry yeast*
1¼ *cups warm (105° to 115° F) water*
   1 *tablespoon honey*
   1 *teaspoon salt*
   1 *tablespoon olive oil*
  ½ *cup whole wheat flour*
3¼ *to 3¾ cups unbleached all-purpose flour*

1. Sprinkle yeast over ¼ cup of the water in large bowl of electric mixer. Add honey. Let stand until yeast is soft (about 5 minutes).

2. Stir in remaining 1 cup water, salt, and oil. Add whole wheat flour and 2 cups unbleached flour. Mix to blend; then beat at medium speed until smooth and elastic (about 5 minutes). Stir in 1 cup more unbleached flour to make a soft dough.

3. Turn dough out onto a floured board or pastry cloth. Knead until springy and small bubbles form just under surface (12 to 15 minutes), adding just enough flour to prevent dough from being sticky.

4. Turn dough in a greased bowl. Cover with plastic wrap and a towel; let rise in a warm place until doubled in bulk (about 1 hour).

5. Punch dough down, cover, and let rest for 10 minutes. Shape into a round ball.

6. Grease an 8- to 9-inch-diameter round or 5- by 8-inch oval (3 to 4 inches deep) basket with a prominent weave. Sprinkle evenly with about 2 tablespoons of the remaining unbleached flour. Place ball of dough in basket. Cover lightly and let rise until almost doubled in bulk (40 to 45 minutes).

7. Preheat oven to 375° F. Carefully turn loaf out onto a greased baking sheet, patterned side up. Bake until bread is golden brown and sounds hollow when tapped (35 to 40 minutes). Cool on wire rack.

Makes 1 round loaf.

NORTH GERMAN FARM BREAD

The German equivalent of French country bread is called *Bauernbrot*. This version is from the city of Bremen. It has a chewy interior and crust—and a sprinkling of oatmeal gives a distinctive appearance.

   2 *packages active dry yeast*
   2 *cups warm (105° to 115° F) water*
   2 *tablespoons brown sugar*
1½ *teaspoons salt*
   2 *tablespoons butter or margarine, softened*
  ½ *cup each quick-cooking rolled oats and whole wheat flour*
4½ *to 5 cups unbleached all-purpose flour*
   1 *egg white, slightly beaten with 2 teaspoons water*

1. Sprinkle yeast over ½ cup of the water in large bowl of electric mixer. Add 1 teaspoon of the brown sugar. Let stand until yeast is soft (about 5 minutes).

2. Stir in remaining 1½ cups warm water, remaining brown sugar, salt, and butter.

3. Measure 2 tablespoons of the rolled oats; set aside for topping. To yeast mixture add remaining 6 tablespoons rolled oats, whole wheat flour, and 3 cups of the unbleached flour. Mix to blend; then beat at medium speed until smooth and elastic (about 5 minutes). Stir in about 1 cup more unbleached flour to make a soft dough.

4. Turn dough out onto a board or pastry cloth coated with some of the remaining ½ to 1 cup unbleached flour. Knead until dough is springy and small bubbles form just under surface (15 to 20 minutes), adding just enough more flour to prevent dough from being sticky.

5. Turn dough in a greased bowl. Cover with plastic wrap and a towel; let rise in a warm place until doubled in bulk (45 minutes to 1 hour).

6. Punch dough down and let rest for 10 minutes. Divide into two equal portions. Shape each into a round ball. Place on greased baking sheets. Brush with egg white mixture; sprinkle with reserved rolled oats. Let rise until almost doubled in bulk (40 to 45 minutes).

7. Preheat oven to 375° F. Bake until loaves are well browned and sound hollow when tapped (40 to 45 minutes). Transfer to wire racks to cool.

Makes 2 round loaves.

Rising in an oval or round basket called a banneton *(shown with radishes) imprints this French Country Bread-in-a-Basket with floury ridges. See opposite page for the recipe.*

45

BLACK FOREST ONION RYE BREAD

The Black Forest is the home of this crisp-outside, moist-inside rye bread, where it is called *Zwiebelbrot*. Let these loaves be the main attraction of a buffet with a variety of sausages and cheeses, mustards, and a tart cucumber salad.

    ¼ cup butter or margarine
    2 medium onions, finely
       chopped
    2 teaspoons caraway seed
    2 packages active dry yeast
    2 cups warm (105° to 115°F)
       water
    2 tablespoons brown sugar
    1½ teaspoons salt
    1½ cups medium rye flour
    4½ to 5 cups bread flour
    1 egg, slightly beaten with
       1 teaspoon water
    2 teaspoons coarse or
       kosher salt

1. Melt butter in a large frying pan over medium heat. Add onion and caraway seed; cook, stirring often, until onion is soft but not browned (6 to 8 minutes). Remove from heat.

2. Sprinkle yeast over ½ cup of the water in large bowl of electric mixer. Add 1 teaspoon of the brown sugar. Let stand until yeast is soft (about 5 minutes).

3. Stir in remaining 1½ cups warm water, remaining brown sugar, salt, and onion mixture.

4. Add rye flour and 2 cups of the bread flour. Mix to blend; then beat at medium speed until smooth and elastic (about 5 minutes). Stir in about 2 cups more bread flour to make a soft dough.

5. Turn dough out onto a floured board or pastry cloth. Knead until dough is springy and small bubbles form just under surface (15 to 20 minutes), adding just enough more flour to prevent dough from being sticky.

6. Turn dough in a greased bowl. Cover with plastic wrap and a towel; let rise in a warm place until doubled in bulk (about 1 hour).

7. Punch dough down, cover, and let rest for 10 minutes. Divide dough into two equal portions. Using the palms of your hands, roll each half on a floured surface into a slender loaf about 14 inches long. Place on greased baking sheets. Let rise until almost doubled in bulk (40 to 45 minutes).

8. Preheat oven to 375° F. Brush loaves lightly with egg mixture. Sprinkle 1 teaspoon of the salt over each loaf. Slash each loaf in three parallel diagonal cuts.

9. Bake until loaves are well browned and sound hollow when tapped (35 to 40 minutes). Transfer to wire racks to cool.

Makes 2 long loaves.

SWEDISH RYE BREAD

Scandinavia is also known for fragrant rye breads. This dark version from Sweden is perfumed with fennel seed, orange rind, and honey.

    2 packages active dry yeast
    1½ cups warm (105° to 115°F)
       water
    ⅓ cup honey
    2 teaspoons instant coffee
       powder or granules
    2 teaspoons salt
       Grated rind of 1 orange
    ¾ teaspoon fennel or anise seed,
       slightly crushed
    2 tablespoons butter or
       margarine, softened
    2 cups medium rye flour
    3½ to 4 cups all-purpose flour
    1 egg white, beaten with 2
       teaspoons water

1. Sprinkle yeast over ½ cup of the warm water in large bowl of electric mixer. Add 1 teaspoon of the honey. Let stand until yeast is soft (about 5 minutes).

2. Dissolve instant coffee in remaining 1 cup warm water; add to yeast mixture with remaining honey, salt, orange rind, fennel or anise seed, and butter. Stir to blend well.

3. Add 1 cup of the rye flour and 2 cups of the all-purpose flour. Mix to blend, then beat at medium speed until smooth and elastic (about 5 minutes). Stir in remaining 1 cup rye flour and about 1 cup more all-purpose flour to make a soft dough.

4. Turn dough out onto a board or pastry cloth coated with some of the remaining ½ to 1 cup all-purpose flour. Knead until dough is springy and small bubbles form just under surface (15 to 20 minutes), adding just enough more flour to prevent dough from being sticky.

5. Turn dough in a greased bowl. Cover with plastic wrap and a towel; let rise in a warm place until doubled in bulk (about 1 hour).

6. Punch dough down, cover with inverted bowl, and let rest for 10 minutes. Divide into two equal portions. Shape each into an oval loaf about 3 by 8 inches. Place on greased baking sheets. Let rise until almost doubled in bulk (35 to 45 minutes).

7. Preheat oven to 375° F. Brush loaves lightly with egg white mixture. Slash diagonally down center of each loaf in three or four places.

8. Bake until loaves are well browned and sound hollow when tapped (35 to 40 minutes). Transfer to wire racks to cool.

Makes 2 oval loaves.

BRAIDS, TWISTS, AND COILS

The ingeniously shaped breads that follow are as much a delight to the eye as to the palate. The simplest is a single strand of dough, coiled into a stylized snail. It is not much more complex to divide the dough into three strands and braid them. But as it bakes, watch that braid puff and swell into a loaf of spectacular dimensions. An alternative is to curve a braid into a wreath, then trim it with squiggly egg-gilded coils. The next step is to fill the strips that comprise each strand, creating a delicious mosaic as the bread is sliced.

COILED LIGHT RYE BREAD

Because it resembles a snail, this delicate rye bread is called *Schneckenbrot* in its home territory of Germany's Black Forest. Bake it to serve with bratwurst in a sauce of sautéed onions.

> 2 packages active dry yeast
> 2 cups warm (105° to 115°F) water
> 1 tablespoon honey
> 1½ teaspoons salt
> 2 tablespoons butter or margarine, softened
> 1½ cups medium rye flour
> 4 to 4½ cups unbleached all-purpose flour

1. Sprinkle yeast over ½ cup of the warm water in large bowl of electric mixer. Add honey. Let stand until yeast is soft (about 5 minutes).

2. Stir in remaining 1½ cups warm water, salt, and butter.

3. Add rye flour and 2½ cups of the unbleached flour. Mix to blend, then beat at medium speed until smooth and elastic (about 5 minutes). Stir in about 1 cup more unbleached flour to make a soft dough.

4. Turn dough out onto a board or pastry cloth coated with some of the remaining unbleached flour.

Knead until dough is springy and small bubbles form just under surface (15 to 20 minutes), adding just enough more flour to prevent dough from being sticky.

5. Turn dough in a greased bowl. Cover with plastic wrap and a towel; let rise in a warm place until almost doubled in bulk (about 1 hour).

6. Punch dough down and divide into two equal portions. Working with one portion at a time, shape into a ball. Then roll dough under palms of your hands on a floured surface into a strand 1½ inches in diameter and 30 inches long. Place one end in center of a greased baking sheet; coil strand round and round into a stylized snail shape, tucking outer end under edge. Let rise until almost doubled in bulk (45 minutes to 1 hour).

7. Preheat oven to 375° F. Bake until loaves are well browned and sound hollow when tapped (40 to 50 minutes). Transfer to wire racks.

Makes 2 round loaves.

This Coiled Light Rye Bread seems all the crustier because the dough is shaped from a single long strand curved round and round to form a stylized snail.

Complement handsome Italian Bread Wreath (a double recipe is pictured) with a flamboyant salad of juicy tomatoes, fresh basil leaves, and triangles of whole-milk mozzarella cheese. The recipe is on the opposite page.

BRAIDED OATMEAL BREAD

This generous loaf serves a large crowd at a salad or casserole buffet. Or, if you wish to offer a variety of after-dinner cheeses, the mild flavor of oatmeal and whole wheat teams well with many different kinds.

    1 cup quick-cooking rolled oats
    1¾ cups water
    1 package active dry yeast
    2 tablespoons honey
    ½ cup warm (105° to 115° F)
       milk
    1½ teaspoons salt
    3 tablespoons butter or
       margarine, softened
    3¾ to 4 cups unbleached
       all-purpose flour
    2 eggs
    1½ cups whole wheat flour

1. Measure 2 tablespoons of the rolled oats; set aside for topping. Bring 1½ cups of the water to a boil; pour over remaining rolled oats in a medium bowl. Let stand until just warm to touch (105° to 115° F).

2. Sprinkle yeast over remaining water in large bowl of electric mixer. Add 1 teaspoon of the honey. Let stand until yeast is soft (about 5 minutes).

3. Stir in rolled oats mixture, milk, remaining honey, salt, and butter.

4. Add 3 cups of the unbleached flour. Mix to blend, then beat at medium speed until smooth and elastic (about 5 minutes). Beat in one of the eggs until well combined. Stir in whole wheat flour and about ¼ cup more unbleached flour to make a soft dough.

5. Turn dough out on a floured board or pastry cloth. Knead until dough is smooth and satiny and small bubbles form just under surface (10 to 12 minutes), adding just enough more unbleached flour to prevent dough from being sticky.

6. Turn dough in a greased bowl. Cover with plastic wrap and a towel; let rise in a warm place until doubled in bulk (about 1 hour).

7. Punch dough down; cover and let rest for 10 minutes. Divide into three portions. Roll each under palms of hands on a lightly floured surface into an 18-inch-long strand. Place the three strands side by side on a large, greased baking sheet. Braid, being careful not to overstretch dough. Pinch ends of braid and tuck under to seal. Let rise until almost doubled in bulk (35 to 45 minutes).

8. Preheat oven to 375° F. Beat reserved egg in a small bowl to blend yolk and white. Brush egg lightly over braid. Sprinkle evenly with reserved 2 tablespoons rolled oats.

9. Bake until braid is golden brown and sounds hollow when tapped (30 to 35 minutes). Transfer to a wire rack to cool.

Makes 1 large loaf.

BRAIDED EGG BREAD

Sesame or poppy seed speckles the crust of this traditional Jewish bread, *challah*. It's a brunch classic with strawberries and your favorite omelet.

    1 package active dry yeast
    1¼ cups warm (105° to 115° F)
        water
    2 teaspoons sugar
    1 teaspoon salt
    2 tablespoons salad oil
    4½ to 5 cups flour
    2 eggs
    1 egg yolk, beaten with ½
        teaspoon water
    3 tablespoons sesame or
        poppy seed

1. Sprinkle yeast over ¼ cup of the water in large bowl of electric mixer. Add sugar. Let stand until yeast is soft (about 5 minutes). Add remaining 1 cup warm water, salt, and oil.

2. Add 3 cups of the flour. Mix to blend, then beat at medium speed until smooth and elastic (about 5 minutes). Beat in eggs, one at a time, then gradually stir in about 1½ cups more flour to make a soft dough.

3. Turn dough out onto a board or pastry cloth coated with some of the remaining flour. Knead until dough is smooth and small bubbles form just under surface (12 to 15 minutes), adding more flour to prevent dough from being sticky.

4. Turn dough in a greased bowl. Cover and let rise in a warm place until doubled in bulk (about 1 hour). Punch down, cover again, and let rise a second time until doubled in bulk (about 45 minutes). Punch dough down and divide into three equal portions.

5. On a lightly floured surface roll each portion into an 18-inch-long strand. Place the three strands side by side diagonally across a large,

greased baking sheet; braid. Pinch ends, tucking under slightly to seal. Let rise until almost doubled in bulk (about 45 minutes). Preheat oven to 375° F. Brush egg yolk mixture lightly over braid. Sprinkle evenly with sesame or poppy seed.

6. Bake until braid is well browned and sounds hollow when tapped lightly (40 to 45 minutes). Slide onto a wire rack to cool.

Makes 1 large loaf.

ITALIAN BREAD WREATH

A specialty of the colorful island of Capri, this bread is trimmed with S-shaped curls of dough. You'll enjoy it with Italian cheeses, singly or in a layered cheese *torta*.

    1 package active dry yeast
    1¾ cups warm (105° to 115° F)
        water
    1 teaspoon sugar
    1 tablespoon salt
    2 tablespoons butter or
        margarine, softened
    6½ to 7 cups flour
    3 eggs

1. Sprinkle yeast over warm water in large bowl of electric mixer. Add sugar. Let stand until yeast is soft (about 5 minutes).

2. Add salt and butter. Stir until salt dissolves.

3. Add 3½ cups of the flour. Mix to blend, then beat at medium speed until smooth and elastic (about 5 minutes). Beat in 2 of the eggs. Then gradually stir in about 2½ cups more flour to make a soft dough.

4. Turn dough out onto a board or pastry cloth coated with some of the remaining ½ to 1 cup flour. Knead until dough is smooth and satiny and small bubbles form just under surface (10 to 15 minutes), adding enough flour to prevent dough from being sticky.

5. Turn dough in a greased bowl. Cover and let rise in a warm place until almost doubled in bulk (1¼ to 1½ hours).

6. Punch dough down and turn out onto a lightly floured surface. Cover with inverted bowl and let rest for 10 minutes.

7. Pinch off and reserve about 1 cup of the dough. Divide remaining dough into two equal portions. Shape each into a strand about 32 inches long, rolling it under palms of hands. Place strands side by side; twist loosely together, then form into a 10-inch wreath on a large, greased baking sheet or pizza pan. Pinch ends together to seal.

8. Divide reserved dough into 10 equal pieces. Roll each under palms into a strand about 10 inches long. Beat remaining egg with 2 teaspoons water to blend yolk and white; brush lightly over bread wreath. Shape each strand of dough into an S-shaped curve. Place curved strands over wreath at evenly spaced intervals. Brush decorations lightly with a little more of the egg.

9. Let bread wreath rise until it looks puffy (30 to 45 minutes). Brush all over with remaining egg, using as much of it as possible.

10. Preheat oven to 400° F. Bake for 20 minutes; reduce heat to 325° F and continue baking until wreath is golden brown and sounds hollow when tapped (25 to 30 minutes). Slide onto a wire rack to cool.

Makes 1 large loaf.

DENA'S ONION BRAID

Paprika-seasoned onions are enclosed in each strand of this braid, twisting invitingly through the poppy seed-sprinkled loaf. It's good at any time of year—with creamy goulash in winter or barbecued steak on a summer evening.

> 1 package active dry yeast
> ¾ cup warm (105° to 115° F) water
> ¼ cup sugar
> 1 cup warm (105 to 115° F) milk
> 1½ teaspoons salt
> ¼ cup butter or margarine, softened
> 4 to 4½ cups flour
> 1 egg, separated
> 1 tablespoon poppy seed

Onion Filling

> ¼ cup butter or margarine
> 1 large onion, finely chopped
> 1 small clove garlic, minced or pressed
> 1 tablespoon poppy seed
> ½ teaspoon sweet Hungarian paprika
> 1 tablespoon grated Parmesan cheese

1. Sprinkle yeast over warm water in large bowl of electric mixer. Add 1 teaspoon of the sugar. Let stand until yeast is soft (about 5 minutes).

2. Add milk, remaining sugar, salt, and butter.

3. Add 2½ cups of the flour. Mix to blend, then beat until smooth and elastic (about 5 minutes). Beat in egg yolk until batter is smooth and well combined.

4. Stir in about 1½ cups more flour to make a soft dough.

5. Turn dough out onto a board or pastry cloth coated with some of the remaining ½ cup flour; knead until dough is smooth and satiny and small bubbles form just under surface (8 to 10 minutes), adding just enough flour to prevent dough from being sticky.

6. Turn dough in a greased bowl. Cover with plastic wrap and a towel; let rise in a warm place until doubled in bulk (1 to 1¼ hours).

7. Punch dough down and turn out onto a lightly floured surface. Cover with inverted bowl and let stand for 10 minutes.

8. Roll out to a 15- by 18-inch rectangle. Cut lengthwise into three strips, each 5 by 18 inches. Spread a third of the Onion Filling down center of each, allowing about a ½-inch margin all the way around. Starting from an 18-inch side, roll each strip, jelly-roll fashion; pinch ends and long edges to seal.

9. Place filled rolls side by side on a large, greased baking sheet; braid, being careful not to overstretch dough. Pinch ends of braid and tuck under slightly to seal.

10. Let rise until almost doubled in bulk (about 45 minutes). Preheat oven to 350° F.

11. Beat reserved egg white in a small bowl with 1 teaspoon water just until blended. Brush egg white mixture lightly over braid. Sprinkle evenly with poppy seed.

12. Bake until braid is golden brown and sounds hollow when tapped (30 to 35 minutes). Slide onto a wire rack to cool.

Makes 1 large loaf.

Onion Filling In a medium frying pan melt butter over moderate to low heat; add onion and cook, stirring occasionally, until soft and lightly browned (8 to 10 minutes). Mix in garlic. Remove from heat and stir in poppy seed, paprika, and Parmesan cheese.

SOME LIKE IT FLAT

While a loaf that rises to plump proportions is the goal of baking most yeast breads, some breads inflate less than others—deliberately. To people who think the crust is the best part of the loaf, such breads couldn't be better—they are almost all crust.

Because these breads are rolled, patted, or stretched out so thinly, the second rising period after they have been shaped is very brief. Just let them stand until they look puffy, usually in less than 15 minutes.

FLAT ITALIAN ONION BREAD

Slathered with herb-tinged onions sautéed in olive oil, this savory bread is great with broiled or grilled steak or lamb chops.

Two variations using the same dough are possible. The first is a Roman-style bread baked in a big, flat pan. It's drizzled with olive oil and crusted with Parmesan cheese. For the second, divide the dough into six rounds. Dimpled with melted pools of Gorgonzola cheese, the bread is so good with red wine that you might choose it to accompany a tasting of several Italian varieties.

> 1 package active dry yeast
> 1 cup warm (105° to 115° F) water
> 2 tablespoons honey
> 2 tablespoons olive oil
> ½ teaspoon salt
> 2¾ to 3¼ cups bread flour

Onion Topping

> 2 tablespoons butter or margarine
> 2 tablespoons olive oil
> 2 medium onions, thinly sliced and separated into rings
> ½ teaspoon dried sage

1. Sprinkle yeast over water in large bowl of electric mixer. Add 1 teaspoon of the honey. Let stand until yeast is soft (about 5 minutes).

2. Mix in the remaining honey, oil, and salt.

3. Add 2 cups of flour. Mix to blend, then beat for 5 minutes at medium speed, until dough is elastic and pulls away from sides of bowl. Stir in about ½ cup more flour to make a soft dough.

4. Turn dough out onto a floured board or pastry cloth. Knead until smooth and elastic and small bubbles form just under surface (12 to 15 minutes), adding just enough flour to prevent dough from being sticky.

5. Place dough in a greased bowl, cover, and let rise until doubled in bulk (about 1 hour).

6. Punch dough down. Cover with inverted bowl and let rest for 10 minutes. Divide dough in half. Roll and stretch each portion out to a circle about 12 inches in diameter. Place on greased baking sheets or pizza pans. Spoon half the topping over each round, brushing with olive oil from frying pan. Let stand until dough looks puffy (12 to 15 minutes).

7. Preheat oven to 425° F. Bake until golden brown (15 to 20 minutes). Cut into wedges and serve hot.

Makes 2 flatbreads (12 to 16 servings).

Onion Topping In a large frying pan over medium-low heat, heat butter with oil. Add onions; cook, stirring occasionally, until soft but not browned (15 to 20 minutes). Stir in sage. Remove from heat.

Focaccia or Pizza Bianca After dough has risen, been punched down, and rested in step 6, roll and stretch into a large rectangle. Press into a greased, shallow 10- by 15-inch baking pan. Make depressions in dough, using your thumb or the end of a wooden spoon, at 1-inch intervals. Brush lightly with 3 tablespoons olive oil, then sprinkle evenly with ⅓ cup grated Parmesan cheese.

Let stand until dough looks puffy (12 to 15 minutes). Preheat oven to 425° F and bake until well browned (15 to 20 minutes). Cut into strips and serve hot.

Makes 1 large flatbread.

Gorgonzola Pizzette After dough has risen, been punched down, and rested for 10 minutes in step 6, divide into six equal portions. Roll and stretch each portion to a circle about 6 inches in diameter. Place on two large, greased baking sheets. Make depressions in dough, using your thumb or the end of a wooden spoon, at 1-inch intervals. Brush rounds lightly with olive oil, using about 2 tablespoons in all. Sprinkle evenly with ½ cup crumbled Gorgonzola or other blue-veined cheese. Let stand until dough looks puffy (10 to 12 minutes). Preheat oven to 425° F and bake until golden brown (12 to 15 minutes). Serve hot.

Makes 6 small flatbreads.

Flat Italian Onion Bread (opposite page) is shown with two variations, Focaccia and Gorgonzola Pizzette.

OLIVE OIL FOUGASSE WITH OLIVES

Based on a Provençale specialty, these flatbreads have an intriguing shape that invites breaking off irregular pieces. Serve them with a main-dish *salade Niçoise*.

   1 *package active dry yeast*
   ½ *cup warm (105° to 115° F) water*
   2 *teaspoons sugar*
   ½ *cup warm (105° to 115° F) milk*
   ¼ *cup olive oil*
   ¼ *teaspoon salt*
  2¾ *to 3 cups unbleached all-purpose flour*
   ¼ *cup chopped green (not stuffed) olives*

1. Sprinkle yeast over ¼ cup of the warm water in large bowl of electric mixer. Add sugar. Let stand until yeast is soft (about 5 minutes).

2. Stir in remaining ¼ cup warm water, milk, 3 tablespoons of the olive oil, and salt.

3. Add 2 cups of the unbleached flour. Mix to blend, then beat at medium speed until dough is elastic and pulls away from sides of bowl (about 5 minutes). Stir in olives, then about ½ cup more flour to make a soft dough.

4. Turn dough out onto a board or pastry cloth coated with some of the remaining ¼ to ½ cup flour. Knead until dough is smooth and satiny and small bubbles form just under surface (10 to 12 minutes), adding just enough flour to prevent dough from being sticky.

5. Turn dough in a greased bowl. Cover with plastic wrap and a towel; let rise in a warm place until doubled in bulk (45 minutes to 1 hour).

6. Punch dough down. Cover and let rest for 10 minutes. Divide into two equal portions. Roll and stretch each portion out to a rectangle about 8 by 10 inches. Place on greased baking sheets. With a sharp knife make six to eight evenly spaced diagonal slashes in two rows, cutting all the way through dough. Open these slits by pulling them well apart.

7. Brush loaves lightly with remaining 1 tablespoon olive oil. Let stand until dough looks puffy (12 to 15 minutes).

8. Preheat oven to 425° F. Bake until golden brown (15 to 20 minutes). Serve warm.

Makes 2 flatbreads (12 to 16 servings).

HERB-CRUSTED SCHIACCIATA

The Italian verb *schiacciare* means to squash or flatten, and that's just what happens to this wheaty bread (pronounce it skee-ah-CHA-tah). Cut in wedges and served warm, it's wonderful with a thick bean soup.

   1 *package active dry yeast*
   ½ *cup warm (105° to 115° F) water*
   2 *tablespoons sugar*
   ½ *cup warm (105° to 115° F) milk*
   ¼ *cup olive oil*
   ½ *teaspoon salt*
  2¼ *to 2½ cups unbleached all-purpose flour*
   ½ *cup whole wheat flour*
   ½ *teaspoon dried rosemary*
   ⅛ *teaspoon each dried sage and thyme*
   1 *teaspoon coarse or kosher salt*

1. Sprinkle yeast over ¼ cup of the warm water in large bowl of electric mixer. Add 1 teaspoon of the sugar. Let stand until yeast is soft (about 5 minutes).

2. Stir in remaining ¼ cup warm water, milk, remaining sugar, 2 tablespoons of the olive oil, and salt.

3. Add 1½ cups of the unbleached flour and whole wheat flour. Mix to blend, then beat for 5 minutes at medium speed, until dough is elastic and pulls away from sides of bowl. Stir in about ½ cup more unbleached flour to make a stiff dough.

4. Turn dough out onto a board or pastry cloth coated with some of the remaining ¼ to ½ cup unbleached flour. Knead until dough is smooth and satiny and small bubbles form just under surface (10 to 12 minutes), adding just enough flour to prevent dough from being sticky.

5. Turn dough in a greased bowl. Cover with plastic wrap and a towel; let rise in a warm place until doubled in bulk (45 minutes to 1 hour).

6. Meanwhile, heat remaining 2 tablespoons olive oil in a small pan over low heat with rosemary, sage, and thyme until warm to the touch. Remove from heat and let stand while dough rises.

7. Punch risen dough down. Cover and let rest for 10 minutes. Divide into two equal portions. Roll and stretch each portion out to a circle about 12 inches in diameter. Place on greased baking sheets or pizza pans.

8. Brush rounds of dough with olive oil–herb mixture, dividing it evenly. Sprinkle each with ½ teaspoon of the coarse salt. Let stand until dough looks puffy (15 to 20 minutes).

9. Preheat oven to 425° F. Bake until well browned (12 to 15 minutes). Serve hot, cut into wedges.

Makes 2 flatbreads (12 to 16 servings).

Chopped green olives flavor Olive Oil Fougasse (opposite page), a French flatbread that complements the colorful salade Niçoise.

menu

CORNED BEEF AND RYE BREAD SUPPER

Glazed Corned Beef With Simmered Lentils

Dilled Coleslaw

New York Corn Rye Bread and Butter

Apples-in-Cream Torte

Light Red Wine or Beer

Coffee

Corned-beef-on-rye is a classic delicatessen combination, and it's also the inspiration for a hearty supper that is much more sophisticated than most deli fare.

While corned beef simmers to tenderness, bake plump, cornmeal-crusted loaves of fragrant rye bread. The corned beef is finished in the oven with a Mustard-Honey Glaze while the lentils cook in some of the flavorful corned beef stock.

GLAZED CORNED BEEF WITH SIMMERED LENTILS

- 3½- to 4-pound corned beef brisket
- 1 medium onion, thinly slivered
- 1 medium carrot, chopped
- 1 stalk celery, thinly sliced
- 1 clove garlic, minced or pressed
- 1 tablespoon mixed pickling spices, tied in a square of cheesecloth
- ¼ cup prepared chili sauce
- 2 cups (about 12 oz) dried lentils
  Chopped parsley

Mustard-Honey Glaze

- ¼ cup firmly packed brown sugar
- ½ teaspoon ground ginger
- 3 tablespoons Dijon mustard
- ¼ cup honey

1. Rinse corned beef well under cold running water, then place in a 5- to 6-quart kettle or Dutch oven. Cover with 8 cups water and bring to a boil over medium-high heat. Drain, discarding water. Add onion, carrot, celery, garlic, and pickling spices; pour in enough water to cover.

2. Bring to a boil; cover, reduce heat, and simmer until corned beef is very tender (about 3 hours). Remove meat from cooking liquid, reserving liquid. Discard pickling spices.

3. Preheat oven to 350° F. Place corned beef, fat side up, on a rack in a roasting pan. Spoon glaze over corned beef. Bake, uncovered, until well browned (30 to 40 minutes).

4. Meanwhile, measure 3 cups of the cooking liquid (including some of the vegetables) and return it to kettle in which corned beef cooked. Mix in 3 cups water and chili sauce. Bring to a boil over medium-high heat. Add lentils, reduce heat, and boil gently, uncovered, until lentils are tender and most of the liquid is absorbed (30 to 35 minutes). Slice corned beef thinly; serve with lentils; sprinkle with parsley.

Serves 6 to 8.

Mustard-Honey Glaze In a small bowl mix brown sugar and ginger. Blend in mustard and honey.

NEW YORK CORN RYE BREAD

- 2 packages active dry yeast
- 2 cups warm (105° to 115° F) water
- 3 tablespoons sugar
- ½ cup warm (105° to 115°F) milk
- 2 teaspoons salt
- 1 tablespoon caraway seed
- 2 tablespoons salad oil
- 4 to 4½ cups bread flour
- ½ cup yellow cornmeal
- 2 cups medium rye flour
- 1 egg white, beaten with 1 teaspoon water

1. Sprinkle yeast over ½ cup of the warm water in large bowl of electric mixer. Add 1 teaspoon of sugar. Let stand until soft (about 5 minutes).

2. Stir in remaining 1½ cups warm water, milk, remaining sugar, salt, caraway seed, and oil.

3. Add 3 cups of the bread flour. Mix to blend, then beat at medium speed until smooth and elastic (about 5 minutes). Cover with plastic wrap and a towel; let stand in a warm place until bubbly (about 20 minutes).

4. Set aside 3 tablespoons of the cornmeal for topping; to batter add remaining cornmeal. Then stir in rye flour and about ½ cup more bread flour to make a soft dough.

5. Turn dough out onto a floured board or pastry cloth. Knead until dough is springy and small bubbles form just under surface (15 to 20 minutes), adding just enough flour to prevent dough from being sticky.

6. Turn dough in a greased bowl. Cover with plastic wrap and a towel; let rise in a warm place until doubled in bulk (about 1 hour).

7. Punch dough down, cover, and let rest for 10 minutes. Divide dough into two equal portions. Roll each into a ball. Place on greased baking sheets coated with some of the reserved cornmeal. Brush generously on all sides with egg white mixture. Sprinkle with remaining cornmeal. Let rise until almost doubled in bulk (30 to 45 minutes).

8. Preheat oven to 350° F. Bake until loaves are well browned and sound hollow when tapped (45 to 50 minutes). Transfer to wire racks to cool.

Makes 2 round loaves.

DILLED COLESLAW

    1 medium head (about 1½ lbs)
       green cabbage, thinly
       shredded
    6 green onions (use part of
       tops), thinly sliced
    1 sweet red or green bell pepper,
       seeded and finely chopped
    ½ cup sour cream
    ¼ cup mayonnaise
    1 small clove garlic, minced
       or pressed
    2 tablespoons finely chopped
       fresh dill or 1 teaspoon dried
       dill weed
    1 tablespoon each lemon juice
       and white wine vinegar
    ½ teaspoon salt
    ⅛ teaspoon ground white pepper
    3 tablespoons salad oil
       Chopped fresh dill, for garnish

1. In a large bowl combine cabbage, green onions, and bell pepper.

2. In a medium bowl mix until smooth sour cream, mayonnaise, garlic, dill, lemon juice, vinegar, salt, sugar, and white pepper. Using a whisk or fork, gradually beat in oil until well combined.

3. Mix dressing lightly with cabbage mixture. Cover and refrigerate for 1 to 2 hours to blend flavors.

4. Serve sprinkled with dill.

Serves 6 to 8.

APPLES-IN-CREAM TORTE

    4 medium-sized tart cooking
       apples, peeled, cored,
       and sliced
    2 packages (3 oz each)
       cream cheese, softened
    ¾ cup sugar
    1 teaspoon vanilla extract
    ½ teaspoon grated lemon rind
    ¼ teaspoon ground nutmeg
    2 eggs
    ½ cup half-and-half

Pecan Press-In Pastry

 1¼ cups flour
    ¼ cup ground pecans (whirl in
       blender or food processor
       until powdery)
    ⅓ cup sugar
    ½ cup cold butter or margarine
    1 egg yolk
    ½ teaspoon vanilla extract

1. Press Pecan Press-In Pastry into bottom and halfway up sides of a 9-inch springform pan. Arrange apple slices evenly in prepared pastry shell.

2. In a medium bowl beat cream cheese until fluffy; beat in sugar, vanilla, lemon rind, and nutmeg. Add eggs, one at a time, beating well after each addition. Blend in half-and-half. Pour mixture over apples.

3. Preheat oven to 400° F. Bake until apples are tender and pastry is well browned (45 to 55 minutes). Place pan on a wire rack. Cool to room temperature; remove pan sides. Cut in wedges to serve.

Serves 6 to 8.

Pecan Press-in Pastry In a medium bowl mix flour, pecans, and sugar. Cut in butter until crumbly. Beat egg yolk with vanilla. Stir egg mixture into flour mixture. Press dough together into a flattened ball.

MAKING SOURDOUGH BREAD

Thanks to the Gold Rush, sourdough bread is a specialty of San Francisco and other cities in the West. For the prospectors, who had no access to food stores, saving some of the yeasty batter for the next day's baking was a necessity.

Although most of us no longer live in such circumstances, the tangy flavor, chewy texture, and appealing crust of breads baked from a sourdough starter are reasons enough to make one and use it often.

The Care and Feeding of a Sourdough Starter

The bacteria needed for sourdough fermentation are present in many milk products. This starter is made from packaged dry yeast and nonfat milk. Once you get the starter under way, add more milk and flour every time you use it to keep it going.

Replenish your starter using equal parts of flour and warm (105° to 115° F) milk. If, for example, you've used 1 cup of the starter in a recipe, blend in 1 cup each of flour and warm milk. Then cover the starter and let it stand in a warm place for several hours or overnight until it's again active and bubbly.

Between uses, refrigerate the starter in a tightly covered container. Bring the starter to room temperature before using it again. Leaving it out overnight before baking in the morning is usually convenient.

If you use the starter regularly—at least every 10 to 14 days—it should last indefinitely. Some sourdough starters, according to baking lore, are passed from one generation of family bakers to the next!

SOURDOUGH STARTER

When you replenish the milk and flour after using your starter, be sure to use the same kind—nonfat milk and all-purpose flour—as in the original mixture.

- *1 package active dry yeast*
- *1 cup warm (105° to 115° F) water*
- *1 cup warm (105° to 115° F) nonfat milk*
- *2 cups flour*

1. Sprinkle yeast over water in a medium bowl; stir until dissolved. Mix in warm milk.

2. Add flour; mix to blend, then beat until smooth.

3. Transfer mixture to a 2-quart glass, pottery, enamel, or stainless steel container. Cover tightly and let stand at room temperature (75° to 85° F) until mixture smells sour (24 to 48 hours); stir down frequently or as needed (mixture will be quite active for several hours after it is prepared).

4. Use starter (stir down before measuring) or refrigerate until ready to use (up to 1 week). After each use, replenish as directed below. Use starter at room temperature.

Makes about 2 cups.

Sourdough Baking

Traditionally, loaves of sourdough bread are plump and round, with the top crust scored in a tic-tac-toe design. But you can also form this dough into any of the shapes suggested for French Bread (see page 58). The bread is leavened both by the starter and by a package of dry yeast; for this reason, baking the bread won't be overly time-consuming. One good way to keep your prized starter lively is to make Sourdough Pancakes (see opposite page) once every weekend.

SOURDOUGH BREAD

Monterey jack cheese is a traditional complement to San Francisco-style sourdough bread, but it is also good in all kinds of sandwiches and for toast.

- *1 cup Sourdough Starter (at left)*
- *1 package active dry yeast*
- *2 cups warm (105° to 115° F) water*
- *2 teaspoons each sugar and salt*
- *5 to 5½ cups all-purpose flour*
- *2 cups bread flour Cornmeal*
- *1 teaspoon cornstarch, blended with ⅓ cup water*

1. Let starter come to room temperature.

2. Sprinkle yeast over ¼ cup of the warm water in large bowl of electric mixer. Add sugar. Let stand until soft (about 5 minutes).

3. Stir in remaining 1¾ cups water, salt, and starter.

4. Add 4 cups of the all-purpose flour. Mix to blend, then beat at medium speed until smooth and elastic (about 5 minutes).

5. Gradually beat in bread flour, then add about ½ cup more all-purpose flour to make a stiff dough.

6. Turn dough out onto a board or pastry cloth coated with some of the remaining ½ to 1 cup flour. Knead until dough is springy and small bubbles form just under surface (15 to 20 minutes), adding just enough more flour to prevent dough from being sticky.

7. Turn dough in a greased bowl. Cover with plastic wrap and a towel; let rise in a warm place until doubled in bulk (about 1 hour).

8. Punch dough down; cover with inverted bowl and let rest for 10 minutes. Divide into two equal portions. Shape each into a ball and place on greased baking sheets that have been lightly dusted with cornmeal. Let rise until almost doubled in bulk (45 minutes to 1 hour). Preheat oven to 400° F.

9. Bring cornstarch mixture to a boil in a small pan over medium-high heat, stirring until thick and clear. Brush each loaf with warm cornstarch mixture. With a razor blade cut a crosshatch design about ½ inch deep in the top of each loaf.

10. Bake until loaves are golden brown and sound hollow when tapped (30 to 35 minutes). Slide onto wire racks to cool.

Makes 2 loaves.

SOURDOUGH PANCAKES

Crisp on the outside and moist within, these tangy pancakes are good with syrup, honey, or butter-sautéed apple slices and powdered sugar.

> ½ cup *Sourdough Starter (see opposite page)*
> ½ cup each *warm (105° to 115° F) water and warm milk*
> 1¼ cups *flour*
> ¼ teaspoon *salt*
> ½ teaspoon *baking soda*
> 1 tablespoon *sugar*
> 1 *egg*
> 3 tablespoons *butter or margarine, melted and cooled*

1. Let starter come to room temperature in a large bowl.

2. Blend in the water and milk. Add flour; stir until most of the lumps are gone. Cover and let stand at room temperature (75° to 85° F) or in a barely warm oven, if room is cold, until the next day.

3. Just before making pancakes, blend in salt, baking soda, and sugar. In a small bowl beat egg and butter; add to sourdough mixture and mix to blend well.

4. Place greased or seasoned pancake griddle over medium heat until a few drops of water dance on the hot surface. Using a scant ¼ cup batter for each pancake, pour batter onto the hot griddle.

5. Cook pancakes on one side until they are puffed, full of bubbles, and dry at edges. Turn pancakes and cook until second side is golden brown. Serve at once with butter and syrup.

Makes about 1 dozen 4-inch pancakes, 3 to 4 servings.

Crusty Sourdough Bread is a familiar sight to San Franciscans. Now you can make the tangy starter and have your own tempting loaves in the traditional round shape whenever you like.

57

TRADITIONAL FRENCH BREAD

As anyone who has eaten even the simplest meal in France will attest, bread is one of the glories of the French table. It is present at every meal—golden and crisply crusted—with an irresistibly appetizing aroma.

Creating such a loaf in your own kitchen is a goal for every dedicated baker of bread. Here's a recipe that produces a convincingly French *baguette*—the long, slender loaf with high proportion of crust to crumb. For those who have been tantalized by the variety of other forms of bread seen in the *boulangeries* of the French countryside, the recipe also includes six inventive variations for shaping the dough.

FRENCH BREAD

This recipe contains no fat of any kind and only a little sugar, so the bread it produces is very lean. It will taste best when it's freshly baked (within an hour or less of baking). To freshen it, sprinkle with a little water and reheat in the oven. Or freeze it (see page 9) as soon as it cools; to reheat, let it stand at room temperature for about 15 minutes, then warm it in a 350° F oven.

1 *package active dry yeast*
2 *cups warm (105 to 115° F)*
  water
1 *teaspoon sugar*
2 *teaspoons salt*
5½ *to 6 cups unbleached*
  all-purpose flour

1. Sprinkle yeast over ¼ cup of the warm water in large bowl of electric mixer. Add sugar. Let stand until yeast is soft (about 5 minutes).

2. Stir in remaining 1¾ cups water and salt. Add 4 cups of the flour. Mix to blend; then beat at medium speed until smooth and elastic (about 5 minutes).

3. Gradually beat in about 1 cup more flour to make a soft dough.

4. Turn dough out onto a board or pastry cloth floured with some of the remaining ½ to 1 cup flour. Knead until dough is springy and small bubbles form just under surface (10 to 15 minutes), adding just enough more flour to prevent dough from being sticky.

5. Turn dough in a greased bowl. Cover with plastic wrap and a towel; let rise in a warm place until doubled in bulk (about 1 hour).

6. Punch dough down; knead dough lightly into a ball. Cover with inverted bowl and let rest for 10 minutes. Shape as directed to make one or more of the following variations.

Baguettes Divide dough into three equal portions. Shape each into a slender oval loaf 16 to 18 inches long by rolling the ball of dough under palms of hands to elongate it. Place in greased baguette pans or well apart on a large, greased baking sheet. Let rise until puffy but not quite doubled (20 to 25 minutes). Preheat oven (see Baking Directions). With a razor blade make three diagonal slashes, about ½ inch deep, down center of each loaf.

Makes 3 loaves.

French Rolls or Mexican Bolillos Divide dough into 18 equal portions. Knead and roll each into a ball, then use the palms of both hands to roll from either side to taper and elongate the ends (each roll should be about 5 inches long and 2 inches wide at center). Place shaped rolls well apart on greased baking sheets. Let rise until puffy but not quite doubled (15 to 20 minutes). Preheat oven (see Baking Directions). Using a razor blade, slash each roll down center about ½ inch deep, almost from end to end.

Makes 18 rolls.

Épi (Sheaf of Wheat) Divide dough into three equal portions. Shape each into a slender oval loaf 16 inches long (as for Baguettes). Place loaves well apart on a greased baking sheet. Cutting on the diagonal, slice loaf apart at equal intervals to divide it into 6 sections. Pull every other section out at a 90-degree angle; pinch ends into points. Let rise until puffy but not quite doubled (20 to 25 minutes). Preheat oven (see Baking Directions).

Makes 3 loaves.

Étoile (Daisy) Divide dough into 18 equal portions. Knead and roll each into a ball, then shape 16 of them as for French Rolls. Place one round roll in center of each of two greased baking sheets. Around it arrange eight tapered rolls, radiating out from center like petals of a flower. Let rise until puffy but not quite doubled (15 to 20 minutes). Preheat oven (see Baking Directions). Using a razor blade slash each roll down center about ½ inch deep, almost from end to end.

Makes 2 loaves.

Heart Divide dough into two equal portions. Shape each into a slender strand about 30 inches long, rolling the ball of dough under palms of hands to elongate it smoothly. On each of two greased baking sheets, curve strand into a heart with ends meeting at top; heart should measure about 10 inches from top to bottom. Pinch ends together to seal. Let rise until puffy but not quite doubled (20 to 25 minutes). Preheat oven (see Baking Directions).

Makes 2 loaves.

Couronne (Ring) Divide dough into two equal portions. Shape each into a slender strand about 25 inches long, rolling the ball of dough under palms of hands to elongate it smoothly. On each of two greased baking sheets, curve strand into a circle; pinch ends together to seal. Let rise until puffy but not quite doubled (20 to 25 minutes). Preheat oven (see Baking Directions). Using a razor blade, slash each loaf, making 6 to 8 diagonal cuts about ½ inch deep, radiating out from inner edge.

Makes 2 loaves.

Pain de Brie Divide dough into two equal portions. Shape each into a ball, then roll under palms to make a plump oval about 5 by 9 inches. Place well apart on a large, greased baking sheet. Let rise until puffy but not quite doubled (25 to 30 minutes). Preheat oven (see Baking Directions). Using a razor blade, slash each loaf from end to end, making five or six parallel cuts about ½ inch deep.

Makes 2 loaves.

Baking Directions

For Baguettes, French Rolls, Épi, Étoile, Heart, or Couronne, preheat oven to 450° F. For Pain de Brie, preheat oven to 425° F. Before baking use an atomizer filled with cold water to spray shaped loaves with a fine film of moisture. Place in oven, then spray twice more at 3-minute intervals. Bake until bread is well browned (25 to 30 minutes in all; 30 to 35 minutes for Pain de Brie). Slide onto wire racks to cool.

Baguettes (upper left) are just one possibility for shaping crisp-crusted French Bread. Others are (clockwise from upper left) Couronne (above baguettes), Pain de Brie, Étoile, Épi, Heart, and French Rolls.

ROLLS—THE LITTLEST LOAVES

Dinner rolls and sandwich rolls call for the same baking techniques as yeast loaves. But instead of getting just one loaf or two from each batch of dough, you'll get dozens of rolls.

Bake generous amounts of the rolls in this section, then fill your freezer and serve them for all kinds of occasions, from holiday dinners to summer barbecues.

GOLDEN DINNER ROLLS

One basic dough can be formed into four varieties. Shape all the rolls alike, or try two or three different kinds.

>   2 packages active dry yeast
> ½ cup warm (105° to 115° F) water
> ⅓ cup sugar
> ¾ cup warm (105° to 115° F) milk
>   1 teaspoon salt
> ¼ cup butter or margarine, softened
>   5 to 5½ cups flour
>   2 eggs
>   Melted butter or margarine

1. Sprinkle yeast over the water in large bowl of electric mixer. Add 1 tablespoon of the sugar. Let stand until yeast is soft (about 5 minutes).

2. Add the remaining sugar, milk, salt, and butter.

3. Mix in 2½ cups of the flour; beat until smooth and elastic (about 5 minutes). Beat in eggs, one at a time. Then stir in about 2 cups more flour to make a soft dough.

4. Turn dough out onto a board or pastry cloth coated with some of the remaining ½ to 1 cup flour. Knead until dough is smooth and satiny and small bubbles form just under surface (8 to 10 minutes), adding just enough flour to prevent dough from being sticky.

5. Turn dough in a greased bowl. Cover with plastic wrap and a towel. Let rise in a warm place until doubled in bulk (about 1 hour), or refrigerate (6 to 8 hours, up to 2 days).

6. Punch dough down. Knead into a smooth ball; cover with inverted bowl and let rest for 10 minutes. Shape into one or more of the types of rolls shown on page 61. Place on baking sheets or in baking pans as directed.

7. Let rise until almost doubled in bulk (30 to 45 minutes; 1 to 1¼ hours if dough has been refrigerated). Preheat oven to 400° F.

8. Brush rolls lightly with melted butter. Bake until golden brown (12 to 15 minutes). Transfer to wire racks to cool. If you wish, brush warm rolls with a little more melted butter to give a softer crust.

Makes about 2 dozen rolls.

Parker House Rolls Roll dough out to ¼-inch thickness on a lightly floured surface. Brush with melted butter. Cut into 2½- to 3-inch circles. Use handle of a wooden spoon to make a depression just off center across each circle. Fold along depression and place on greased baking sheets with larger portion on top.

Cloverleaf Rolls Pinch off pieces of dough and shape into 1-inch balls. Dip into melted butter, then place three balls in each cup of a greased 2½-inch muffin pan.

Bowknots Divide dough into 24 equal portions; roll each portion with your hands on a lightly floured surface to make a strand 6 inches long. Tie loosely into a knot. Place on greased baking sheets.

Fantans Roll dough out to about ⅛-inch thickness on a lightly floured surface. Brush with melted butter. Cut dough into strips 1 inch wide. Stack 6 strips on top of one another; cut stacked strips into 1½-inch pieces. Place each stack horizontally in cup of greased 2½-inch muffin pan.

UMBRIAN WALNUT ROLLS

A delicacy during the fall when wine grapes are harvested, *pane di Assisi* is delicious with cheese and red wine or split and filled with prosciutto or other sliced meat to make a light sandwich.

>   2 packages active dry yeast
> ½ cup warm (105° to 115° F) water
> ⅓ cup sugar
> 1½ cups warm (105° to 115° F) milk
> 1½ teaspoons salt
> ¼ teaspoon coarsely ground black pepper
> ⅓ cup olive oil
> 5¾ to 6¼ cups unbleached all-purpose flour
>   1 egg, separated
> ⅔ cup finely chopped walnuts
> ½ cup grated Parmesan cheese
>   2 teaspoons water

1. Sprinkle yeast over the ½ cup warm water in large bowl of electric mixer. Add 1 tablespoon of the sugar. Let stand until yeast is soft (about 5 minutes).

2. Add the remaining sugar, milk, salt, pepper, and oil.

3. Add 4 cups of the flour, mix to blend, then beat at medium speed until smooth and elastic (about 5 minutes).

4. Beat in egg yolk, then blend in walnuts and cheese. Stir in about 1¼ cups more flour to make a soft dough.

5. Turn dough out onto a board or pastry cloth coated with some of the remaining ½ to 1 cup flour. Knead until dough is smooth and satiny and small bubbles form just under surface (8 to 10 minutes), adding just enough flour to prevent dough from being sticky.

6. Turn dough in a greased bowl. Cover with plastic wrap and a towel. Let rise in a warm place until doubled in bulk (about 1 hour).

7. Punch dough down. Cover with inverted bowl and let rest for 10 minutes. Divide into 24 equal pieces. Roll each on a lightly floured surface into a ball.

8. Place rolls about 1 inch apart on greased baking sheets. Flatten each ball slightly. Let rise until almost doubled in bulk (about 30 minutes). Preheat oven to 400° F.

9. Beat egg white with the 2 teaspoons water. Brush rolls lightly with egg white mixture. Bake until well browned (15 to 20 minutes). Transfer to wire racks to cool.

Makes 2 dozen rolls.

Golden Dinner Rolls (opposite page) can take one or more of these four shapes: Bowknots, Parker House Rolls, Cloverleaf Rolls, or Fantans.

Spiral Whole Wheat Bread Sticks are delicious as an appetizer with ripe melon wedges and thinly sliced cold meats, such as rustic salami and Swiss-style air-dried beef (Bündnerfleisch).

WHOLE WHEAT BREAD STICKS

Italian bakers gave the world a civilizing gift when they invented bread sticks. In restaurants in Italy, each table is set with bread sticks, on which diners nibble until the food arrives. Here's a dough that can be shaped in two ways: into plain, straight sticks or into more intricate twists that seem even crisper.

    1 package active dry yeast
    ⅔ cup warm (105° to 115° F)
       water
    1 tablespoon sugar
    ½ teaspoon salt
    ¼ cup olive oil
    2 to 2¼ cups all-purpose flour
    ½ cup whole wheat flour
    1 egg white, beaten with
       1 teaspoon water

1. Sprinkle yeast over the water in large bowl of electric mixer. Add sugar. Let stand until yeast is soft (about 5 minutes).

2. Add salt and oil. Add 1½ cups of the all-purpose flour; mix to blend. Then beat at medium speed until smooth and elastic (about 5 minutes).

3. Stir in whole wheat flour and about ¼ cup more all-purpose flour to make a stiff dough.

4. Turn dough out onto a board or pastry cloth coated with some of the remaining ¼ to ½ cup all-purpose flour. Knead until dough is smooth and satiny and small bubbles form just under surface (about 5 minutes), adding just enough flour to prevent dough from being sticky.

5. Turn dough in a greased bowl. Cover with plastic wrap and a towel. Let rise in a warm place until doubled in bulk (45 minutes to 1 hour).

6. Punch dough down. Cover with inverted bowl and let rest for 10 minutes. Divide into halves, then cut each half into 18 pieces. Using palms of hands, roll each piece into strands about 8 inches long.

7. Place strands parallel and about ½ inch apart on greased baking sheets. Let rise until strands look puffy (15 to 20 minutes). Preheat oven to 325° F.

8. Brush bread sticks lightly with egg white mixture. Bake until crisp and lightly browned (35 to 40 minutes). Transfer to wire racks to cool.

Makes 3 dozen bread sticks.

Braided Bread Sticks Roll each piece of dough into a very thin strand about 16 inches long. Cut into 2 equal strands; twist loosely together. Pinch ends together to seal.

EGG BAGELS

Bagels differ from most rolls in that they're immersed in boiling water before baking. This helps to give them their glossy finish and chewy interior. If you like you can replace up to 2 cups of the all-purpose flour with whole wheat or rye flour.

> 2 packages active dry yeast
> 2 cups warm (105° to 115° F) water
> 2 tablespoons sugar
> 2 teaspoons salt
> ¼ cup salad oil
> 6½ to 7 cups all-purpose flour
> 2 eggs
> 1 cup bread flour
> 8 cups water mixed with 2 tablespoons sugar
> 2 egg yolks, beaten with 1 tablespoon water
> Poppy seed, sesame seed, coarse or kosher salt, or caraway seed

1. Sprinkle yeast over ½ cup of the warm water in large bowl of electric mixer. Add 1 tablespoon of the sugar. Let stand until yeast is soft (about 5 minutes).

2. Add the remaining sugar, remaining 1½ cups water, salt, and oil.

3. Add 4 cups of the all-purpose flour, mix to blend, then beat at medium speed until smooth and elastic (about 5 minutes).

4. Beat in eggs, one at a time, beating until smooth after each addition. Then stir in bread flour and about 2 more cups of the all-purpose flour to make a stiff dough.

5. Turn dough out onto a board or pastry cloth coated with some of the remaining ½ to 1 cup flour. Knead until dough is smooth and satiny and small bubbles form just under surface (about 10 minutes), adding just enough flour to prevent dough from being sticky.

6. Turn dough in a greased bowl. Cover with plastic wrap and a towel. Let rise in a warm place until doubled in bulk (45 minutes to 1 hour).

7. Punch dough down. Cover with inverted bowl and let rest for 10 minutes.

8. Divide into quarters, then divide each quarter into 6 equal portions. Shape each portion into a round ball. To shape, place both your thumbs at the center of one ball of dough. Press them through to make a hole, then use 2 fingers to enlarge the hole and smooth the dough into a doughnut-shaped roll ¾ to 1 inch thick all the way around. As each bagel is shaped, set aside on a lightly floured surface, covering lightly until all are shaped. Let stand until bagels look puffy (15 to 20 minutes).

9. Bring water-sugar mixture to a boil in a wide, deep kettle. Preheat oven to 400° F. Drop bagels into the boiling water, one at a time. They will rise quickly to the surface; boil 3 or 4 at a time so as not to crowd. As each bagel rises to the surface, turn it over. After turning, boil each one an additional 3 minutes.

10. Use a slotted spoon to remove bagels to greased baking sheets, placing slightly apart. Brush bagels with egg yolk mixture. Sprinkle lightly with poppy seed or other topping.

11. Bake until crust is richly browned (25 to 30 minutes). Transfer to wire racks to cool.

Makes 2 dozen bagels.

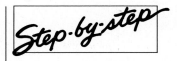

HOW TO MAKE BAGELS

To give Egg Bagels their distinctive shape, glossy finish, and chewy texture, follow the three steps below.

1. Divide dough into balls of equal size. Make a hole in each by pressing your thumbs through center, then shape into a smooth ring.

2. When shaped bagels have risen slightly, drop, one at a time, into boiling water. After boiling, remove with a slotted spoon.

3. Before baking, brush bagels lightly with beaten egg yolks. Finish with a sprinkling of sesame, poppy, or caraway seed.

HAMBURGER OR HOT DOG BUNS

One persuasive school of thought holds that a hamburger or hot dog is only as good as the roll in which it nestles. For such purists, here is a recipe for homemade ones. Keep a supply in the freezer to use as needed.

> 2 *packages active dry yeast*
> ½ *cup warm (105° to 115° F) water*
> ⅓ *cup sugar*
> 1½ *cups warm (105° to 115° F) milk*
> 2 *teaspoons salt*
> ⅓ *cup butter or margarine, softened*
> 6 *to 6½ cups flour*
> 1 *egg*
> *Melted butter or margarine*

1. Sprinkle yeast over the water in large bowl of electric mixer. Add 1 tablespoon of the sugar. Let stand until yeast is soft (about 5 minutes).

2. Add the remaining sugar, milk, salt, and butter.

3. Add 4 cups of the flour, mix to blend, then beat at medium speed until smooth and elastic (about 5 minutes). Beat in egg. Then stir in about 1½ cups more flour to make a soft dough.

4. Turn dough out onto a board or pastry cloth coated with some of the remaining ½ to 1 cup flour. Knead until dough is smooth and satiny and small bubbles form just under surface (8 to 10 minutes), adding just enough flour to prevent dough from being sticky.

5. Turn dough in a greased bowl. Cover with plastic wrap and a towel. Let rise in a warm place until doubled in bulk (about 1 hour).

6. Punch dough down. Knead into a smooth ball; let rest for 10 minutes. Divide into 24 equal pieces. Roll each on a lightly floured surface either into a ball (for hamburger buns) or into a strand 6 inches long (for hot dog buns).

7. Place rolls well apart on greased baking sheets. If making hamburger buns, flatten each ball to a circle about 4 inches in diameter. Let rise until almost doubled in bulk (about 30 minutes). Preheat oven to 400° F.

8. Brush rolls lightly with melted butter. Bake until golden brown (15 to 20 minutes). Transfer to wire racks to cool. Split when cool.

Makes 2 dozen rolls.

KAISER ROLLS

As a change from conventional sandwich rolls, try these crusty German ones sprinkled with poppy or sesame seed. They taste wonderful with hamburgers or ham and Swiss cheese.

> 2 *packages active dry yeast*
> 2 *cups warm (105° to 115° F) water*
> ¼ *cup sugar*
> 2 *teaspoons salt*
> ⅓ *cup salad oil*
> 6 *to 6½ cups flour*
> 1 *egg white, beaten with 2 teaspoons water*
> *Poppy seed or sesame seed*

1. Sprinkle yeast over ½ cup of the warm water in large bowl of electric mixer. Add 1 tablespoon of the sugar. Let stand until yeast is soft (about 5 minutes).

2. Add the remaining sugar, the remaining 1½ cups warm water, salt, and oil.

3. Add 4 cups of the flour, mix to blend, then beat at medium speed until smooth and elastic (about 5 minutes).

4. Stir in about 1½ cups more flour to make a soft dough.

5. Turn dough out onto a board or pastry cloth coated with some of the remaining ½ to 1 cup flour. Knead until dough is smooth and satiny and small bubbles form just under surface (10 to 15 minutes), adding just enough flour to prevent dough from being sticky.

6. Turn dough in a greased bowl. Cover with plastic wrap and a towel. Let rise in a warm place until doubled in bulk (45 minutes to 1 hour).

7. Punch dough down. Cover with inverted bowl and let rest for 10 minutes. Divide into 16 equal pieces. Shape each into a ball.

8. Place rolls about 1 inch apart on greased baking sheets. Let rise until almost doubled in bulk (about 30 minutes). Preheat oven to 400° F.

9. Brush rolls lightly with egg white mixture. Sprinkle with poppy seed or sesame seed. With a razor blade or thin-bladed, sharp knife, slash top of each roll, starting from center and making five evenly spaced cuts about ½ inch deep.

10. Bake until well browned (18 to 20 minutes). Transfer to wire racks to cool.

Makes 16 rolls.

Distinctive Kaiser Rolls turn ground beef patties with your favorite garnishes into a memorable Saturday-night supper.

Flaky homemade Croissants (page 97) greet the day in style, as do many of the tempting sweet breads in this chapter.

Sweet Yeast Breads

Baking yeast coffee cakes
and sweet rolls could be
construed as making a good
thing better—enriching the dough with
sugar, eggs, and butter, then lavishing
it with spices, nuts, raisins,
and other treats. The myriad forms that these
special occasion breads can take
make them as much fun
for the baker who shapes them
as for those who partake of them.
Whether in dramatic rings,
braids, or other ornately shaped loaves
for a large group, or in plump
individual buns, such
sweet breads offer unlimited
creative possibilities.

COFFEE CAKES

When serving brunch or coffee to a large group, the accomplished bread baker's motto might be, "Let them eat coffee cake." From this selection you're sure to find several that will become favorites.

These breads differ from the more standard loaves not only in their more intricate forms, but in the richer doughs from which they are shaped as well. Using more sugar, shortening, and eggs produces doughs that take somewhat longer to rise than their plainer counterparts in the Yeast Breads and Rolls chapter.

LUSCIOUS ALMOND BRAID

A ribbon of ground almond filling spins through each strand of this generously proportioned coffee cake.

2 packages active dry yeast
½ cup warm (105 to 115° F) water
½ cup sugar
¾ cup warm (105 to 115° F) milk
1 teaspoon each salt and vanilla extract
¼ cup butter or margarine, softened
5 to 5½ cups flour
2 eggs
1 egg white, beaten with 1 teaspoon water
Sliced almonds, for decoration

Almond Filling

1½ cups unblanched almonds
¼ cup fine dry bread crumbs
¾ cup sugar
¼ cup butter or margarine, melted
¾ teaspoon almond extract
½ teaspoon vanilla extract
1 egg, slightly beaten

Almond Icing

1 cup confectioners' sugar
1 teaspoon butter or margarine, softened
⅛ teaspoon almond extract
4 teaspoons warm water

1. Sprinkle yeast over the water in large bowl of electric mixer. Add 1 tablespoon of sugar. Let stand until yeast is soft (about 5 minutes).

2. Add the remaining sugar, milk, salt, vanilla, and butter.

3. Add 2½ cups of the flour. Mix to blend, then beat at medium speed until smooth and elastic (about 5 minutes). Beat in eggs, one at a time, beating until smooth after each addition. Stir in about 2 cups more flour to make a soft dough.

4. Turn dough out onto a board or pastry cloth coated with some of the remaining ½ to 1 cup flour. Knead until dough is smooth and satiny and small bubbles form just under surface (15 to 20 minutes), adding just enough flour to prevent dough from being sticky.

5. Turn dough in a greased bowl. Cover with plastic wrap and a towel; let rise in a warm place until doubled in bulk (1 to 1½ hours). While dough rises, prepare Almond Filling.

6. Punch dough down. Cover with inverted bowl and let rest for 10 minutes.

7. Divide dough into three equal portions. Roll each out to a 6- by 18-inch rectangle. Spread a third of the filling down center of each, leaving about a ½-inch margin all the way around. Starting from an 18-inch side, roll each strip, jelly-roll fashion; pinch ends and long edges to seal.

8. Place filled rolls side by side on a large, greased baking sheet; braid, being careful not to stretch strands. Pinch ends of braid and tuck under slightly to seal.

9. Let rise until almost doubled in bulk (35 to 45 minutes). Preheat oven to 350° F.

10. Brush braid lightly with egg white mixture. Bake until braid is richly browned and sounds hollow when tapped (35 to 45 minutes). Slide carefully onto a wire rack. Drizzle warm braid with Almond Icing; decorate with sliced almonds. Let cool to room temperature before slicing.

Makes 1 large coffee cake.

Almond Filling Whirl almonds in food processor or blender until powdery. Mix almonds, crumbs, and sugar to combine thoroughly. Stir in butter and almond and vanilla extracts. Mix in egg to moisten mixture evenly.

Almond Icing Mix all ingredients in a small bowl until smooth.

BUTTERSCOTCH BUBBLE LOAF

Serve this spectacular-looking coffee cake informally, pulling apart the caramel-glazed spheres with fingers—or two forks.

1 package active dry yeast
¼ cup warm (105 to 115° F) water
¼ cup sugar
½ cup warm (105 to 115° F) milk
½ teaspoon salt
1 teaspoon vanilla extract
¼ cup butter or margarine
3¼ to 3½ cups flour
2 eggs

Butterscotch Glaze

¼ cup butter or margarine, softened
½ cup firmly packed brown sugar

Brown Sugar Mixture

½ cup firmly packed
 brown sugar
½ teaspoon ground cinnamon
½ cup finely chopped pecans

1. Sprinkle yeast over the water in large bowl of electric mixer. Add 1 teaspoon of the sugar. Let stand until yeast is soft (about 5 minutes).

2. Add remaining sugar, milk, salt, vanilla, and 2 tablespoons of the butter.

3. Add 1½ cups of the flour. Mix to blend, then beat at medium speed until smooth and elastic (about 5 minutes). Beat in eggs, one at a time. Stir in about 1½ cups more flour to make a soft dough.

4. Turn dough out onto a board or pastry cloth coated with some of the remaining ¼ to ½ cup flour. Knead until dough is smooth and satiny and small bubbles form just under surface (10 to 12 minutes), adding just enough flour to prevent dough from being sticky.

5. Turn dough in a greased bowl. Cover with plastic wrap and a towel; let rise in a warm place until doubled in bulk (1¼ to 1½ hours). While dough rises, prepare Butterscotch Glaze and Brown Sugar Mixture.

6. Punch dough down. Cover with inverted bowl and let rest for 10 minutes. Melt the remaining 2 tablespoons butter.

7. Spread Butterscotch Glaze in greased 5- by 9-inch loaf pan. Divide dough into 24 equal pieces. Shape each piece into a smooth ball.

8. Arrange half of the balls in a single layer in prepared pan; drizzle with half of the melted butter; sprinkle with half of the Brown Sugar Mixture. Cover with remaining balls of dough in a second layer; drizzle with remaining butter and sprinkle with remaining Brown Sugar Mixture. Let rise until almost doubled in bulk (30 to 45 minutes). Preheat oven to 375° F.

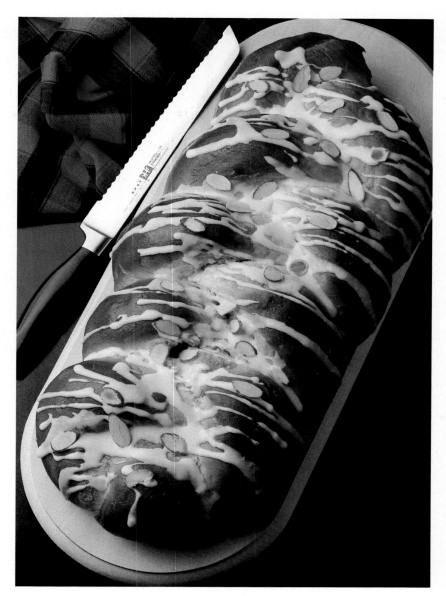

9. Bake until coffee cake is richly browned (25 to 30 minutes). Invert pan carefully onto a serving plate. Let stand with pan in place for 30 seconds, then remove pan. Serve warm or at room temperature.

Makes 1 coffee cake.

Butterscotch Glaze In a medium bowl beat butter with brown sugar until fluffy and well combined.

Brown Sugar Mixture In a small bowl mix brown sugar, cinnamon, and pecans until well combined.

Three almond-filled strands intertwine to make Luscious Almond Braid. The recipe is on the opposite page.

Afternoon tea or coffee goes nicely with slices of fudge and nut-filled Chocolate-Swirled Babka loaf.

CHOCOLATE-SWIRLED BABKA

Streusel-topped and bursting with a fudgy cocoa filling, these rich, sweet loaves are a New York bakery favorite.

> 2 packages active dry yeast
> ½ cup warm (105 to 115° F) water
> ⅓ cup sugar
> ⅔ cup warm (105 to 115° F) milk
> ½ teaspoon each *salt and vanilla extract*
> 3 tablespoons butter or margarine, softened
> 4½ to 5 cups flour
> 3 eggs
> 3 tablespoons butter or margarine, melted
> 1 cup coarsely chopped walnuts

Cocoa Filling

> ⅓ cup unsweetened cocoa
> ⅔ cup sugar

Streusel Topping

> 2 tablespoons butter or margarine, softened
> ¼ teaspoon ground cinnamon
> ⅓ cup confectioners' sugar
> ¼ cup flour

1. Sprinkle yeast over the water in large bowl of electric mixer. Add 1 teaspoon of the sugar. Let stand until yeast is soft (about 5 minutes).

2. Add the remaining sugar, milk, salt, vanilla, and the softened butter.

3. Add 2½ cups of the flour. Mix to blend, then beat at medium speed until smooth and elastic (about 5 minutes). Separate one of the eggs; reserve white for glaze. Beat in egg yolk and whole eggs, one at a time. Stir in about 1½ cups more flour to make a soft dough.

4. Turn dough out onto a board or pastry cloth coated with some of the remaining ½ to 1 cup flour. Knead until dough is smooth and satiny and small bubbles form just under surface (10 to 12 minutes), adding just enough flour to prevent dough from being sticky.

5. Turn dough in a greased bowl. Cover with plastic wrap and a towel; let rise in a warm place until doubled in bulk (45 minutes to 1 hour).

6. Punch dough down. Cover with inverted bowl and let rest for 10 minutes.

7. Divide dough in half. Roll each half out on a floured surface to a 10- by 20-inch rectangle. Brush half of the melted butter over each rectangle of dough, leaving about a ½-inch margin on all edges. Sprinkle half of the Cocoa Filling evenly over buttered surface of each rectangle, then sprinkle each rectangle with half of the nuts.

8. Starting with a 20-inch side, roll each rectangle of dough tightly, jelly-roll fashion. Pinch edge to seal.

9. Zigzag each roll back and forth to fit into a well-greased 4½- by 8½-inch loaf pan.

10. Let rise until almost doubled in bulk (35 to 45 minutes). Preheat oven to 350° F. Beat reserved egg white with 1 teaspoon water; brush egg white mixture over loaves. Sprinkle each loaf with half of the Streusel Topping.

11. Bake until coffee cakes are well browned (30 to 35 minutes). Carefully remove loaves from pans and let cool on wire racks.

Makes 2 coffee cakes.

Cocoa Filling In a small bowl mix cocoa and sugar until well combined and no lumps remain.

Streusel Topping In a medium bowl beat butter with cinnamon until fluffy; gradually beat in sugar, then mix in flour until crumbly and uniformly combined.

ALMOND PRALINE COFFEE CAKE

In France a praline is an almond encased in crisp, caramelized sugar. Buying pralines on a brisk autumn day from a street vendor with his bubbling copper caldron is a happy memory for many tourists. Another version of praline made by French confectioners has a pink candy coating. This bread, a specialty of the town of Bourges in the Loire valley, can be made with either kind. You can also use the familiar butter-toffee almonds or pink or white candy-coated almonds.

> 2 *packages active dry yeast*
> ½ *cup warm (105 to 115° F) water*
> ½ *cup sugar*
> 1 *cup warm (105 to 115° F) milk*
> 1 *teaspoon each salt and vanilla extract*
> ½ *cup butter or margarine, softened*
> 5½ *to 6¼ cups flour*
> 2 *eggs*
> 1 *cup caramelized, candy-coated, or butter-toffee almonds, coarsely chopped*
> 1 *egg, beaten with 1 tablespoon water*

1. Sprinkle yeast over the water in large bowl of electric mixer. Add 1 tablespoon of the sugar. Let stand until yeast is soft (about 5 minutes).

2. Add the remaining sugar, milk, salt, vanilla, and butter.

3. Add 2½ cups of the flour. Mix to blend, then beat at medium speed until smooth and elastic (about 5 minutes). Cover and let stand until light and foamy (20 to 25 minutes).

4. Beat in eggs, one at a time, beating until smooth after each addition. Stir in about 3 cups more flour to make a soft dough.

5. Turn dough out onto a board or pastry cloth coated with some of the remaining ½ to ¾ cup flour. Knead until dough is smooth and satiny and small bubbles form just under surface (10 to 12 minutes), adding just enough flour to prevent dough from being sticky.

6. Turn dough in a greased bowl. Cover with plastic wrap and a towel; let rise in a warm place until doubled in bulk (45 minutes to 1 hour).

7. Punch dough down. Cover with inverted bowl and let rest for 10 minutes.

8. Divide dough into four equal portions. Shape each into a ball. Sprinkle 2 tablespoons of the chopped almonds over bottom of each of two well-greased, round cake pans, 8 inches in diameter. Flatten a portion of dough to an 8-inch circle and place in prepared pan; sprinkle evenly with ¼ cup more of the chopped almonds. Flatten a second portion of dough to make an 8-inch circle and place over the first. Repeat in second pan with remaining two portions of dough and another ¼ cup almonds.

9. Let rise until almost doubled in bulk (35 to 40 minutes). Preheat oven to 350° F.

10. Lightly brush egg mixture generously over tops of coffee cakes. Divide the remaining chopped almonds over the tops of the two coffee cakes, pressing in lightly. Bake until cakes are well browned (40 to 45 minutes). Cool coffee cakes in pans on wire racks for about 10 minutes, then remove carefully and continue cooling cakes on racks. Serve warm or at room temperature.

Makes 2 coffee cakes.

FRENCH EGG BREAD RING

A specialty of the Drôme region of France, *pogne de Romans* is an elegant, cakelike loaf to serve warm with red currant jelly.

    1 package active dry yeast
    ¼ cup warm (105° to 115° F)
       water
    ⅓ cup granulated sugar
    ¼ teaspoon salt
    1 tablespoon orange
       flower water
    ⅓ cup butter or margarine,
       softened
    3¼ to 3½ cups flour
    3 eggs
    ½ teaspoon each confectioners'
       sugar and water

1. Sprinkle yeast over warm water in large bowl of electric mixer. Add 1 teaspoon of the granulated sugar. Let stand until yeast is soft (about 5 minutes).

2. Add the remaining granulated sugar, salt, orange flower water, butter, and 1 cup of the flour; mix to blend, then beat at medium speed until smooth and elastic (about 3 minutes).

3. Separate one of the eggs; reserve white for glazing bread, then beat the 2 whole eggs and the egg yolk into dough (one at a time) until well combined. Stir in about 2 cups more flour to make a soft dough.

4. Turn dough out onto a board or pastry cloth coated with some of the remaining ¼ to ½ cup flour. Knead until dough is smooth and satiny and small bubbles form just under surface (10 to 12 minutes), adding just enough flour to prevent dough from being sticky.

5. Turn dough in a greased bowl. Cover with plastic wrap and a towel; let rise in a warm place until doubled in bulk (1½ to 2 hours).

6. Punch dough down, then shape into a smooth ball. Place on a large, greased baking sheet. Flatten to make a circle about 1 inch thick. Cut a 1-inch X in center with scissors or a knife. Use your hands to pull dough away from center, smoothing and shaping dough into a ring with a center area 3½ inches in diameter. Let rise until almost doubled in bulk (30 to 40 minutes). Preheat oven to 350° F.

7. In a small bowl beat reserved egg white with confectioners' sugar and water until well mixed and a little frothy. Brush generously over ring. Slash diagonally, cutting from center to outer edge, in about eight places.

8. Bake until ring is well browned (25 to 30 minutes). Slide onto a wire rack to cool.

Makes 1 coffee cake.

SUGAR-CRUSTED YEAST GALETTE

Another sweet bread of French origin is this big, buttery flatbread. It comes from the walled medieval city of Pérouges, near Lyon.

    ¾ cup butter or margarine
    1 package active dry yeast
    ¼ cup warm (105° to 115° F)
       water
    ½ cup sugar
    1 teaspoon grated lemon rind
    1 egg
    ⅛ teaspoon salt
    1¾ cups flour

1. Soften ½ cup of the butter.

2. Sprinkle yeast over the water in a small bowl. Add 1 tablespoon of the sugar. Let stand until yeast is soft (about 5 minutes).

3. In large bowl of electric mixer, cream the ½ cup softened butter with 2 tablespoons more of the sugar until fluffy; blend in lemon rind, then egg. Stir salt into yeast mixture; blend into butter mixture. Gradually blend in flour to make a soft dough.

Continue beating until dough is smooth and elastic (about 5 minutes).

4. Place dough in a greased bowl. Cover with plastic wrap and a towel and let rise in a warm place until doubled in bulk (about 1½ hours). Stir dough down. Preheat oven to 425° F.

5. Roll dough on a well-floured surface into a circle about 12 inches in diameter. Grease a 16-inch pizza pan. Pat and stretch dough to fit pan. Press into pan, pinching edge of dough to make a slightly raised rim. Cut the remaining ¼ cup butter into 24 equal pieces; distribute evenly over dough. Sprinkle with the remaining 5 tablespoons sugar.

6. Bake until well browned (12 to 15 minutes). Cut into wedges and serve warm.

Makes 1 large, flat coffee cake.

GERMAN WALNUT COFFEE RING

Baked in an angel food cake pan, this handsome German *Nuss-Kranz* brightens coffee *klatsches* in the Mosel River town of Trier.

    1 package active dry yeast
    ¼ cup warm (105° to 115° F)
       water
    ¼ cup sugar
    ¾ cup warm (105° to 115° F)
       milk
    ½ teaspoon salt
    1 teaspoon vanilla extract
    ¼ cup butter or margarine,
       softened
    3½ to 3¾ cups flour
    3 egg yolks

Spiced Walnut Filling

    2 cups walnuts
    ⅔ cup sugar
    1½ teaspoons ground cinnamon
    ¼ cup butter or
       margarine, melted
    1 teaspoon vanilla extract
    1 egg, slightly beaten

Powdered Sugar Icing

¾ cup confectioners' sugar
1 teaspoon butter or margarine, softened
¼ teaspoon vanilla extract
1 to 1½ tablespoons warm water

1. Sprinkle yeast over the water in large bowl of electric mixer. Add 1 teaspoon of the sugar. Let stand until yeast is soft (about 5 minutes).

2. Add the remaining sugar, milk, salt, vanilla, and butter.

3. Add 2 cups of the flour, mix to blend, then beat at medium speed until smooth and elastic (about 5 minutes). Beat in egg yolks, one at a time. Stir in about 1¼ cups more flour to make a soft dough.

4. Turn dough out onto a board or pastry cloth coated with some of the remaining ¼ to ½ cup flour. Knead until dough is smooth and satiny and small bubbles form just under surface (10 to 12 minutes), adding just enough flour to prevent dough from being sticky.

5. Turn dough in a greased bowl. Cover with plastic wrap and a towel; let rise in a warm place until doubled in bulk (about 1 hour). Punch dough down. Cover with inverted bowl and let rest for 10 minutes.

6. Roll dough out on a floured surface to make a 16-inch square. Spread with Spiced Walnut Filling, leaving a ½-inch margin on all edges. Starting at one side, roll up jelly-roll fashion; pinch to seal edge. Cut roll into 1-inch slices.

7. Place slices, on edge, in a well-greased, 10-inch angel food cake pan; overlap slices, pulling every other one to outside edge of pan (slices between should be pulled to inside edge of pan). Let rise until almost doubled in bulk (40 to 50 minutes). Preheat oven to 375° F.

8. Bake until coffee cake is richly browned (35 to 40 minutes). Let stand in pan on a wire rack for 10 minutes. Then remove pan sides and tube; transfer cake to rack.

While warm, drizzle with Powdered Sugar Icing and sprinkle with 1 tablespoon ground walnuts (reserved from filling). Let cool to room temperature before slicing to serve.

Makes 1 large coffee cake.

Spiced Walnut Filling Preheat oven to 350° F. Spread walnuts in a shallow pan. Bake until they are golden brown and smell fragrant (10 to 12 minutes). Let cool slightly, then place all the walnuts in food processor (or half the walnuts at a time in blender); process or whirl until finely chopped. Set aside 1 tablespoon chopped walnuts for decoration. In a medium bowl combine sugar and cinnamon. Mix in the remaining chopped walnuts, butter, and vanilla. Then blend in egg.

Powdered Sugar Icing In a small bowl combine sugar, butter, and vanilla. Gradually blend in water until icing is smoothly mixed and of a good consistency for drizzling.

Big, flat Sugar-Crusted Yeast Galette (opposite page) is shown before and after baking. Cut into pie-shaped wedges to serve.

Encrusted with sugar and filberts, Swiss Apple Ring (opposite page) has a spicy dried-apple-and-raisin filling.

POPPY SEED KRINGLE

Use your blender or food processor to grind the poppy seed for this puffy, pretzel-shaped coffee cake. Stores that sell nuts, grains, and spices in bulk are a good source for the quantity of poppy seed needed.

 1 package active dry yeast
 ¼ cup warm (105° to 115°F) water
 ¼ cup sugar
 ½ cup warm (105° to 115°F) milk
 ½ teaspoon salt
 ⅛ teaspoon ground cardamom
 2 tablespoons butter or margarine
 3 to 3¼ cups flour
 2 eggs
 2 tablespoons sliced almonds
 Powdered Sugar Icing (see page 73)

Poppy Seed Filling

 ⅔ cup (about 3 oz) poppy seed
 ½ cup milk
 ¼ cup honey
 ½ cup golden raisins
 ½ teaspoon ground cinnamon
 2 teaspoons grated lemon rind
 ½ teaspoon vanilla extract

1. Sprinkle yeast over the water in large bowl of electric mixer. Add 1 tablespoon of the sugar. Let stand until yeast is soft (about 5 minutes).

2. Add remaining sugar, milk, salt, cardamom, and butter.

3. Add 1½ cups of the flour. Mix to blend, then beat at medium speed until smooth and elastic (about 5 minutes). Separate one of the eggs; reserve white for glaze, then beat whole egg and egg yolk into dough until well combined. Stir in about 1 cup more flour to make a soft dough.

4. Turn dough out onto a board or pastry cloth coated with some of the remaining ½ to ¾ cup flour. Knead until dough is smooth and satiny and small bubbles form just under surface (12 to 15 minutes), adding just enough flour to prevent dough from being sticky.

5. Turn dough in a greased bowl. Cover with plastic wrap and a towel; let rise in a warm place until doubled in bulk (1 to 1¼ hours). While dough rises, prepare Poppy Seed Filling.

6. Punch dough down. Cover with inverted bowl and let rest for 10 minutes.

7. Roll dough out on a floured surface into a 6- by 30-inch strip. Spread with cooled filling, leaving about a ½-inch margin all the way around. Fold the 30-inch sides across the filling to meet in center; pinch long edge to seal.

8. Place on a greased baking sheet, sealed edge down. Curve and criss-cross ends to form a pretzel shape, tucking ends under to hold them in place.

9. Let rise until almost doubled in bulk (30 to 45 minutes). Preheat oven to 350° F.

10. Beat reserved egg white with 1 teaspoon water. Brush egg white mixture lightly over coffee cake; sprinkle with almonds. Bake until richly browned (25 to 30 minutes). Slide carefully onto a wire rack. Drizzle warm kringle with icing. Let cool slightly before cutting to serve.

Makes 1 coffee cake.

Poppy Seed Filling Whirl poppy seed, half at a time, in blender until powdery (or process, all at once, in food processor). Place poppy seed in a 1½-quart saucepan with milk, honey, raisins, and cinnamon. Bring to a boil over medium heat; reduce heat and boil gently, stirring occasionally, until thick (8 to 10 minutes). Remove from heat, stir in lemon rind and vanilla, and let cool to room temperature.

SWISS APPLE RING

A luscious dried-apple filling with golden raisins wends its spicy way through this appealing breakfast bread.

    1 package active dry yeast
    ¼ cup warm (105° to 115° F) water
    ¼ cup sugar
    ¾ cup warm (105° to 115° F) milk
    ½ teaspoon salt
    1 teaspoon vanilla extract
    ¼ cup butter or margarine, softened
 3¼ to 3½ cups flour
    3 egg yolks
    1 egg white, beaten with ½ teaspoon water
    2 tablespoons coarsely chopped filberts

Dried-Apple Filling

 1½ cups water
    2 cups (6-oz pkg) dried apples
    2 tablespoons lemon juice
    ½ cup sugar
    ½ cup golden raisins
    1 teaspoon grated lemon rind
    ½ teaspoon ground cinnamon
    ¼ teaspoon ground nutmeg

1. Sprinkle yeast over the water in large bowl of electric mixer. Add 1 tablespoon of the sugar. Let stand until yeast is soft (about 5 minutes).

2. Add 1 tablespoon of the sugar (reserve the remaining 2 tablespoons for topping), milk, salt, vanilla, and butter.

3. Add 2 cups of the flour. Mix to blend, then beat at medium speed until smooth and elastic (about 5 minutes). Beat in egg yolks, one at a time. Stir in about 1 cup more flour to make a soft dough.

4. Turn dough out onto a board or pastry cloth coated with some of the remaining ¼ to ½ cup flour. Knead until dough is smooth and satiny and small bubbles form just under surface (10 to 12 minutes), adding just enough flour to prevent dough from being sticky.

5. Turn dough in a greased bowl. Cover with plastic wrap and a towel; let rise in a warm place until doubled in bulk (1¼ to 1½ hours). While dough rises, prepare Dried-Apple Filling.

6. Punch dough down. Cover with inverted bowl and let rest for 10 minutes.

7. Roll dough out on a floured surface to an 18-inch square. Spread with filling, leaving a 1-inch margin on all sides. Roll up jelly-roll fashion; pinch to seal long edge.

8. Place roll, seam side down, on a large, greased baking sheet; curve into a ring. Moisten ends and pinch together to seal. At 2-inch intervals cut slits in dough just to first layer of filling. Let rise until almost doubled in bulk (30 to 45 minutes). Brush lightly with egg white mixture, then sprinkle with the remaining 2 tablespoons sugar and filberts. Preheat oven to 350° F.

9. Bake until coffee cake is richly browned (35 to 40 minutes). Carefully slide onto a wire rack. Serve warm or at room temperature.

Makes 1 coffee cake.

Dried-Apple Filling In a 2-quart saucepan combine water, apples, and lemon juice. Bring to a boil over high heat; reduce heat, cover, and simmer until apples are very tender (20 to 25 minutes). Drain well, then purée apples with sugar in food processor or blender. Transfer purée to a medium bowl; mix in raisins, lemon rind, cinnamon, and nutmeg. Filling should be thick but moist enough to spread.

PINEAPPLE LADDER COFFEE CAKE

This recipe produces two generous coffee cakes. Bake one to enjoy now and another to freeze (see tips on freezing breads, page 9).

  2 packages active dry yeast
  ½ cup warm (105° to 115° F) water
  ½ cup granulated sugar
  ¾ cup warm (105° to 115° F) milk
  1 teaspoon salt
  2 teaspoons grated orange rind
  ⅓ cup butter or margarine, softened
  4¾ to 5¼ cups flour
  2 eggs
  ¼ cup sliced almonds
  Confectioners' sugar

Orange-Pineapple Filling

  1 can (20 oz) pineapple chunks in unsweetened pineapple juice
  ½ cup sugar
  2 tablespoons cornstarch
  1 tablespoon grated orange rind

1. Sprinkle yeast over the water in large bowl of electric mixer. Add 1 teaspoon of the sugar. Let stand until yeast is soft (about 5 minutes).

2. Add remaining sugar, warm milk, salt, orange rind, and butter.

3. Add 2½ cups of the flour. Mix to blend, then beat at medium speed until smooth and elastic (about 5 minutes). Separate one of the eggs; reserve white for glaze, then beat whole egg and egg yolk into dough until well combined. Stir in about 1¾ cups more flour to make a soft dough.

4. Turn dough out onto a board or pastry cloth coated with some of the remaining ½ to 1 cup flour. Knead until dough is smooth and satiny and small bubbles form just under surface (12 to 15 minutes), adding just enough flour to prevent dough from being sticky.

5. Turn dough in a greased bowl. Cover with plastic wrap and a towel; let rise in a warm place until doubled in bulk (1¼ to 1½ hours). While dough rises, prepare Orange-Pineapple Filling.

6. Punch dough down. Cover with inverted bowl and let rest for 10 minutes.

7. Divide dough in half. Roll each portion into a 10- by 15-inch rectangle. Place each on a large, greased baking sheet. Spread half of the filling down center of each, covering about the middle third of the dough in a 3½- by 15-inch strip.

8. With scissors or a sharp knife, make cuts in from the 15-inch sides at about 1½-inch intervals, cutting almost to edge of filling. Bring cut edges over filling, alternating strips to create a lattice effect. Let rise until almost doubled in bulk (about 45 minutes). Preheat oven to 350° F.

9. Beat reserved egg white with 1 teaspoon water. Brush egg white mixture lightly over coffee cakes; sprinkle with almonds, using 2 tablespoons for each cake. Bake until coffee cakes are richly browned (25 to 30 minutes). Slide carefully onto wire racks. Dust lightly with confectioners' sugar while still warm. Serve warm or at room temperature.

Makes 2 coffee cakes.

Orange-Pineapple Filling Drain pineapple, reserving juice. In a 1½- to 2-quart saucepan mix sugar and cornstarch to combine well. Measure ½ cup of the pineapple juice and add it to the sugar mixture. Cook, stirring constantly, over medium heat until thickened and clear. Stir in pineapple and orange rind and cook for 1 minute more. Remove from heat and let cool slightly.

HONEY-AND-ALMOND-GLAZED COFFEE CAKE

Easy to shape in a big rectangular pan, this coffee cake has a baked-on frosting to enhance its fluffy, cakelike texture.

  ⅓ cup golden raisins
  2 tablespoons kirsch or brandy
  1 package active dry yeast
  ¼ cup warm (105° to 115° F) water
  ⅓ cup sugar
  ½ cup warm (105° to 115° F) milk
  ½ teaspoon salt
  ⅓ cup butter or margarine, softened
  3½ to 3¾ cups flour
  2 eggs

Honey-Almond Topping

  ¼ cup butter or margarine, softened
  ½ teaspoon almond extract
  3 tablespoons honey
  1 egg white
  ¾ cup confectioners' sugar
  1 cup slivered almonds

1. In a small bowl combine raisins and kirsch; cover and let stand for several hours or overnight.

2. Sprinkle yeast over the warm water in large bowl of electric mixer. Add 1 tablespoon of the sugar. Let stand until yeast is soft (about 5 minutes).

3. Add the remaining sugar, milk, salt, and butter.

4. Add 1½ cups of the flour. Mix to blend, then beat at medium speed until smooth and elastic (about 5 minutes). Beat in eggs, one at a time, beating until smooth after each addition. Stir in raisin mixture. Stir in about 1¾ cups more flour to make a soft dough.

5. Turn dough out onto a board or pastry cloth coated with some of the remaining ¼ to ½ cup flour. Knead until dough is smooth and satiny and small bubbles form just under surface (10 to 15 minutes), adding just enough flour to prevent dough from being sticky.

6. Turn dough in a greased bowl. Cover with plastic wrap and a towel; let rise in a warm place until doubled (1 to 1¼ hours). While dough rises, prepare topping.

7. Punch dough down. Cover with inverted bowl and let rest for 10 minutes.

8. Roll dough out on a floured surface into a rectangle about 8 by 10 inches. Pat and stretch to fit evenly into a well-greased 9- by 13-inch baking pan. Spread evenly with topping.

9. Let rise until doubled in bulk (20 to 30 minutes). Preheat oven to 350° F.

10. Bake until a deep golden color (30 to 35 minutes). Let cool slightly before cutting into squares to serve.
Makes 1 coffee cake.

Honey-Almond Topping In a medium bowl combine butter, almond extract, and honey; beat until fluffy. Blend in egg white, then gradually add confectioners' sugar, beating until smoothly combined. Stir in almonds.

A lunch or brunch of fresh fruits and iced tea sparkles when you add Lemon Swirl Bundt Coffee Cake. The recipe is on page 78.

LEMON SWIRL BUNDT COFFEE CAKE

Here is a tart, lemon-glazed coffee cake that is quickly made from a batter that requires no kneading. It is good either with brunch or as an accompaniment to a fruit salad supper.

>   2 packages active dry yeast
>   ¼ cup warm (105° to 115°F) water
>   ⅓ cup sugar
>   ½ cup warm (105° to 115°F) milk
>   ¾ teaspoon salt
>   ¼ teaspoon ground nutmeg
>   2 teaspoons grated lemon rind
>   1½ teaspoons vanilla extract
>   ⅔ cup butter or margarine, softened
>   4 cups flour
>   4 eggs
>   Grated lemon rind, for garnish (optional)

Lemon Sugar

>   ⅓ cup sugar
>   2 tablespoons grated lemon rind

Lemon Glaze

>   1 cup confectioners' sugar
>   2 teaspoons butter or margarine, softened
>   ½ teaspoon grated lemon rind
>   1½ to 2 tablespoons lemon juice

1. Sprinkle yeast over the water in large bowl of electric mixer. Add 1 teaspoon of the sugar. Let stand until yeast is soft (about 5 minutes).

2. Add remaining sugar, milk, salt, nutmeg, the 2 teaspoons lemon rind, vanilla, and butter. Then stir in 1½ cups of the flour; mix to blend, then beat until batter is elastic (about 5 minutes).

3. Beat in eggs, one at a time, beating well after each addition. Gradually mix in the remaining 2½ cups flour. Then beat again until batter is elastic (about 5 minutes).

4. Transfer batter to a greased bowl. Cover with plastic wrap and a towel. Let rise in a warm place until doubled in bulk and light (about 1 hour). Prepare Lemon Sugar.

5. Stir batter down; spoon about a third of it into a well-greased, lightly floured 10-inch bundt pan or other fluted tube pan (10- to 12-cup capacity). Sprinkle with half of the Lemon Sugar. Spoon in another third of the batter, then sprinkle with remaining Lemon Sugar. Cover with remaining batter.

6. Let rise until doubled in bulk (about 45 minutes). Preheat oven to 350° F.

7. Bake coffee cake until well browned (30 to 35 minutes). Carefully invert onto a wire rack. Drizzle while warm with Lemon Glaze. If desired, decorate with additional grated lemon rind.

Makes 1 large coffee cake.

Lemon Sugar In a small bowl thoroughly combine sugar and lemon rind, crushing lemon rind with a spoon to release oils.

Lemon Glaze In a small bowl combine confectioners' sugar, butter, and lemon rind. Gradually blend in lemon juice until frosting is smooth and of a good drizzling consistency.

SWEET ROLLS—PETITE TREATS

Some of the most appreciative sounds that ever greet a baker are those evoked by the fragrance of cinnamon buns in the oven and the sight of a tray of shimmering, freshly baked, sticky pecan rolls. Here are recipes for these and other sweet rolls to earn much deserved praise.

THE STICKIEST PECAN ROLLS

Wonderfully gooey through and through, these abundantly nut-filled rolls are also distinguished by a trace of orange and a measure of whole wheat flour in the dough. They are at their most appealing served warm.

>   2 packages active dry yeast
>   ½ cup warm (105° to 115°F) water
>   ¾ cup granulated sugar
>   ½ cup warm (105° to 115°F) milk
>   1 teaspoon salt
>   2 teaspoons grated orange rind
>   ½ cup butter or margarine, softened
>   4½ to 5 cups all-purpose flour
>   2 eggs
>   ½ cup whole wheat flour
>   ½ cup butter or margarine, melted
>   1 cup firmly packed brown sugar
>   1 cup pecan halves
>   1 cup coarsely chopped pecans

Cinnamon Filling

>   1 cup sugar
>   1½ teaspoons ground cinnamon

1. Sprinkle yeast over the water in large bowl of electric mixer. Add 1 tablespoon of the granulated sugar. Let stand until yeast is soft (about 5 minutes).

2. Add remaining granulated sugar, milk, salt, orange rind, and softened butter.

3. Add 3 cups of the all-purpose flour. Mix to blend, then beat at medium speed until smooth and elastic (about 5 minutes). Beat in eggs, one at a time, beating until smooth after each addition. Stir in whole wheat flour, then about 1½ cups more all-purpose flour to make a soft dough.

4. Turn dough out onto a board or pastry cloth coated with some of the remaining ½ cup all-purpose flour. Knead until dough is smooth and satiny and small bubbles form just under surface (12 to 15 minutes), adding just enough flour to prevent dough from being sticky.

5. Turn dough in a greased bowl. Cover with plastic wrap and a towel; let rise in a warm place until doubled in bulk (1¼ to 1½ hours).

6. While dough rises, prepare baking pan. Pour ¼ cup of the melted butter into a 9- by 13-inch baking pan; tip and tilt to coat pan evenly. Sprinkle evenly with brown sugar, then with pecan halves.

7. Punch dough down. Cover with inverted bowl and let rest for 10 minutes. Roll dough out on a floured surface into an 18-inch square. Brush with remaining melted butter. Sprinkle with Cinnamon Filling, then with chopped pecans. Starting from an 18-inch side, roll dough jelly-roll fashion; moisten long edge and pinch to seal. Cut into 12 equal slices.

8. Arrange slices, cut sides down, in prepared baking pan. Cover lightly with waxed paper. Let rise until doubled in bulk (about 1 hour). Preheat oven to 350° F.

9. Bake until well browned (30 to 35 minutes). Let stand in pan on rack for 1 minute; then invert carefully onto a serving tray. Let stand with pan in place for 30 seconds, then remove pan. Serve warm.

Makes 1 dozen rolls.

Cinnamon Filling In a small bowl mix sugar and cinnamon.

Here are the Stickiest Pecan Rolls you'll ever taste, with nuts both inside and out. The recipe begins on the opposite page.

CREAM CHEESE PINWHEELS

The cream cheese filling will remind you of the center of a cheese Danish, but this lemony sweet dough is much easier to prepare.

    1 package active dry yeast
    ¼ cup warm (105° to 115° F)
      water
    ¼ cup sugar
    ½ cup warm (105° to 115° F)
      milk
    ½ teaspoon salt
    1 teaspoon grated lemon rind
    ¼ cup butter or margarine,
      softened
    3 to 3¼ cups flour
    2 eggs
    2 tablespoons butter or
      margarine, melted

Cream Cheese Filling

    1 package (8 oz) cream
      cheese, softened
    1 tablespoon whipping cream
    ¼ cup sugar
    1 teaspoon grated lemon rind
    ½ teaspoon vanilla extract
    ¼ cup golden raisins

1. Sprinkle yeast over the water in large bowl of electric mixer. Add 1 tablespoon of the sugar. Let stand until yeast is soft (about 5 minutes).

2. Add remaining sugar, milk, salt, lemon rind, and the ¼ cup softened butter.

3. Add 1½ cups of the flour. Mix to blend, then beat at medium speed until smooth and elastic (about 5 minutes). Separate one of the eggs, reserving white for glaze. Add egg yolk and whole egg, one at a time, beating until smooth after each addition. Stir in about 1¼ cups more flour to make a soft dough.

4. Turn dough out onto a board or pastry cloth coated with some of the remaining ¼ to ½ cup flour. Knead until dough is smooth and satiny and small bubbles form just under surface (10 to 12 minutes), adding just enough flour to prevent dough from being sticky.

5. Turn dough in a greased bowl. Cover with plastic wrap and a towel; let rise in a warm place until doubled in bulk (1 to 1¼ hours). While dough rises, prepare Cream Cheese Filling.

6. Punch dough down. Cover with inverted bowl and let rest for 10 minutes.

7. Roll dough out on a floured surface into a 12- by 18-inch rectangle. Brush with the 2 tablespoons melted butter. Spread evenly with filling. Starting from an 18-inch side, roll dough jelly-roll fashion; moisten long edge and pinch to seal. Cut roll into 1-inch slices.

8. Arrange slices, cut sides down, in well-greased, 2½-inch muffin pans. Cover lightly with waxed paper. Let rise until doubled in bulk (40 to 45 minutes). Preheat oven to 350° F.

9. In a small bowl beat reserved egg white with 1 teaspoon water. Brush lightly over rolls. Bake until richly browned (25 to 30 minutes). Remove rolls from pans while warm. Serve warm or at room temperature.

Makes 18 rolls.

Cream Cheese Filling In a medium bowl beat cream cheese and cream until fluffy. Blend in sugar, then lemon rind and vanilla. Stir in raisins.

CZECH APRICOT-FILLED ROLLS

These plump, sugar-dusted rounds are sometimes called *kolache*. The fruit filling can also be made with dried prunes.

    2 packages active dry yeast
    ½ cup warm (105° to 115° F)
      water
    ⅓ cup sugar
    1¼ cups warm (105° to 115° F)
      milk
    1 teaspoon salt
    2 teaspoons grated lemon rind
    ½ cup butter or margarine,
      softened
    5½ to 6 cups flour
    2 eggs
      Confectioners' sugar

Apricot Filling

    1 cup dried apricots
    1 cup water
    ½ cup sugar
    1 tablespoon lemon juice
    ½ teaspoon grated lemon rind
    ½ teaspoon ground cinnamon
    ¼ teaspoon ground allspice

1. Sprinkle yeast over the water in large bowl of electric mixer. Add 1 tablespoon of the sugar. Let stand until yeast is soft (about 5 minutes).

2. Add the remaining sugar, milk, salt, lemon rind, and butter.

3. Add 3 cups of the flour. Mix to blend, then beat at medium speed until smooth and elastic (about 5 minutes). Beat in eggs, one at a time, beating until smooth after each addition. Stir in about 2 cups more flour to make a soft dough.

4. Turn dough out onto a board or pastry cloth coated with some of the remaining ½ to 1 cup flour. Knead until dough is smooth and satiny and small bubbles form just under surface (15 to 20 minutes), adding just enough flour to prevent dough from being sticky.

5. Turn dough in a greased bowl. Cover with plastic wrap and a towel; let rise in a warm place until doubled in bulk (1 to 1½ hours). While dough rises, prepare Apricot Filling.

6. Punch dough down. Cover with inverted bowl and let rest for 10 minutes.

7. Divide dough into two equal portions. Roll each half out on a floured surface to about a ½-inch thickness. Cut with a 2½-inch round cutter; transfer circles of dough to greased baking sheets, placing them about 2 inches apart.

8. Let rolls rise until they look puffy (20 to 25 minutes). Preheat oven to 375° F.

9. With back of a teaspoon carefully press down center of each roll to make a hollow. Spoon a generous teaspoon of the Apricot Filling into each hollow.

10. Bake until rolls are golden brown (15 to 20 minutes). Transfer to wire racks to cool. Sprinkle lightly with confectioners' sugar and serve warm or at room temperature.

Makes 30 rolls.

Apricot Filling In a small saucepan combine apricots and water. Place over medium-high heat and bring to a boil; cover, reduce heat, and simmer until apricots are very tender (8 to 10 minutes). Drain, reserving ¼ cup of the reserved cooking liquid. In blender or food processor combine apricots, the ¼ cup liquid, sugar, lemon juice, lemon rind, cinnamon, and allspice. Whirl or process until smooth.

ORANGE–SOUR CREAM TWISTS

Cutting butter into the flour to make this dough results in a delicate, flaky pastry. The twisted, ring-shaped rolls seem so light that no one will want to stop after eating just one!

> 1 package active dry yeast
> ¼ cup warm (105° to 115° F) water
> 1 tablespoon sugar
> 2½ cups flour
> ½ teaspoon salt
> ½ cup cold butter or margarine, diced
> 2 eggs, separated
> ½ teaspoon each *vanilla extract* and *grated orange rind*
> ½ cup sour cream
> ¼ cup butter or margarine, melted
> ¼ cup sliced almonds
> Confectioners' sugar

Orange Sugar

> ½ cup sugar
> 1 tablespoon grated orange rind

1. Sprinkle yeast over the water in a medium bowl. Add sugar. Let stand until yeast is soft (about 5 minutes).

2. In large bowl of electric mixer, stir together flour and salt. Using a pastry blender or two knives, cut in the ½ cup diced butter until mixture resembles coarse crumbs.

3. To yeast mixture add egg yolks (reserve whites for glaze), vanilla, orange rind, and sour cream; beat until blended. Gradually add yeast mixture to flour mixture, mixing until flour is evenly moistened.

4. Turn dough out onto a floured board or pastry cloth and knead just until smooth; shape dough into a flattened ball.

5. Wrap dough in plastic wrap and refrigerate for 3 to 5 hours or until next day.

6. Divide dough into two equal portions; wrap and return one portion to refrigerator while working with the first. Roll each out on a floured surface into a 12- by 18-inch rectangle. Brush with half of the ¼ cup melted butter, then sprinkle with half of the Orange Sugar.

7. Fold rectangle in half crosswise, making a 9- by 12-inch rectangle. Cut into 1- by 9-inch strips. Place one end of each strip on a greased baking sheet. Holding that end in place, twist from opposite end and form into a ring; moisten and pinch ends to seal.

8. Cover rolls lightly with waxed paper and let stand until they look puffy (25 to 30 minutes). Preheat oven to 350° F. Beat the 2 reserved egg whites with 2 teaspoons water. Brush rolls lightly with egg white mixture. Sprinkle with almonds.

9. Bake until rolls are golden brown (20 to 25 minutes). Transfer to wire racks. Sprinkle warm rolls lightly with confectioners' sugar.

Makes 2 dozen small rolls.

Orange Sugar In a small bowl thoroughly combine sugar and orange rind, crushing orange rind with a spoon to release oils.

Rum Buns (opposite page) bring a taste of the Caribbean to brunch, along with strawberry daiquiris, shrimp-filled omelets, and tropical fruits.

CINNAMON-RAISIN WHIRLS

Frosting-drizzled cinnamon buns, generously studded with raisins, are an American Sunday breakfast classic. After you bake these once, you're sure to be rewarded with requests for an encore.

> 2 packages active dry yeast
> ½ cup warm (105° to 115° F) water
> ¾ cup sugar
> ⅔ cup warm (105° to 115° F) milk
> 1 teaspoon salt
> ½ cup butter or margarine, softened
> 5 to 5½ cups flour
> 2 eggs
> ⅓ cup butter or margarine, softened
> 1 cup raisins
> Powdered Sugar Icing (see page 73)

Cinnamon Sugar

> ¾ cup sugar
> 1 tablespoon ground cinnamon

1. Sprinkle yeast over the water in large bowl of electric mixer. Add 1 tablespoon of the sugar. Let stand until yeast is soft (about 5 minutes).

2. Add remaining sugar, milk, salt, and the ½ cup softened butter.

3. Add 3 cups of the flour. Mix to blend, then beat at medium speed until smooth and elastic (about 5 minutes). Separate one of the eggs; reserve white for glaze. Beat in egg yolk and whole egg, one at a time, beating until smooth after each addition. Stir in about 2 cups more flour to make a soft dough.

4. Turn dough out onto a board or pastry cloth coated with some of the remaining ½ cup flour. Knead until dough is smooth and satiny and small bubbles form just under surface (12 to 15 minutes), adding just enough flour to prevent dough from being sticky.

5. Turn dough in a greased bowl. Cover with plastic wrap and a towel; let rise in a warm place until doubled in bulk (1¼ to 1½ hours).

6. Punch dough down. Cover with inverted bowl and let rest for 10 minutes.

7. Roll dough out on a floured surface into a 14- by 18-inch rectangle. Spread evenly with the ⅓ cup softened butter, then sprinkle with Cinnamon Sugar. Sprinkle evenly with raisins. Starting from an 18-inch side, roll dough jelly-roll fashion; moisten a long edge and pinch to seal. Cut roll into 12 equal slices.

8. Arrange slices, cut sides down, in a well-greased 9- by 13-inch baking pan. Cover lightly with waxed paper. Let rise until doubled in bulk (45 minutes to 1 hour). Preheat oven to 375° F.

9. In a small bowl beat reserved egg white with 1 teaspoon water. Brush lightly over rolls. Bake until well browned (25 to 30 minutes). Drizzle warm rolls with Powdered Sugar Icing, then serve warm or at room temperature.

Makes 1 dozen rolls.

Cinnamon Sugar In a small bowl mix sugar and cinnamon until well combined.

RUM BUNS

Rum-soaked currants and a rum icing give these handsome sweet rolls a distinctive flavor. Serve them at brunch to accompany shrimp-filled omelets and fresh tropical fruits.

    ⅓ cup dried currants
    ¼ cup rum
    2 packages active dry yeast
    ½ cup warm (105° to 115° F)
       water
    ⅓ cup sugar
    1 cup warm (105° to 115° F)
       milk
    1 teaspoon salt
    3 tablespoons butter or
       margarine, softened
    4½ to 5 cups flour
    1 egg
    2 tablespoons butter or
       margarine, melted
    ¼ cup sugar
    ¼ teaspoon ground cinnamon
    1 egg white, beaten with 1
       teaspoon water
    2 tablespoons chopped pecans

Rum Glaze

    ¾ cup confectioners' sugar
    1 teaspoon butter or margarine,
       softened
    1½ to 2 tablespoons rum

1. Place currants in a small bowl. Add rum, cover, and let stand while preparing dough.

2. Sprinkle yeast over the water in large bowl of electric mixer. Add 1 tablespoon of the ⅓ cup sugar. Let stand until yeast is soft (about 5 minutes).

3. Add remainder of the ⅓ cup sugar, milk, salt, and softened butter.

4. Add 3 cups of the flour. Mix to blend, then beat at medium speed until smooth and elastic (about 5 minutes). Add egg, beating until smooth. Mix in currant mixture. Stir in about 1½ cups more flour to make a soft dough.

5. Turn dough out onto a board or pastry cloth coated with some of the remaining ½ cup flour. Knead until dough is smooth and satiny and small bubbles form just under surface (15 to 20 minutes), adding just enough flour to prevent dough from being sticky.

6. Turn dough in a greased bowl. Cover with plastic wrap and a towel; let rise in a warm place until doubled in bulk (about 1 hour).

7. Punch dough down. Cover with inverted bowl and let rest for 10 minutes.

8. Roll dough out on a floured surface into a 12- by 18-inch rectangle. Brush with the melted butter. Mix the ¼ cup sugar with cinnamon. Sprinkle sugar mixture over buttered surface. Starting with an 18-inch side, roll dough tightly, jelly-roll fashion. Moisten long edge and pinch to seal. Cut into 12 equal slices.

9. Place slices, cut sides down, in a well-greased, shallow 10- by 15-inch baking pan. Let rise until doubled in bulk (20 to 25 minutes). Preheat oven to 375° F.

10. Brush rolls lightly with egg white mixture. Bake until well browned (25 to 30 minutes). Drizzle with Rum Glaze and sprinkle with pecans. Serve warm or at room temperature.

Makes 1 dozen buns.

Rum Glaze Place sugar and butter in a small bowl. Gradually blend in rum, stirring until smooth and of a good drizzling consistency.

ITALIAN RAISIN BRAIDS

Wine-drenched golden raisins sweetened with brown sugar fill these Piedmontese rolls made from a buttery refrigerator dough.

> 1 package active dry yeast
> 1 cup warm (105° to 115° F) water
> ⅓ cup sugar
> ¾ cup undiluted evaporated milk
> 1 teaspoon salt
> 1 egg
> 5 cups flour
> ¼ cup butter or margarine, melted and cooled
> 1 cup cold butter, diced
> 1 egg, beaten with 1 tablespoon water

Golden Raisin Filling

> 2 tablespoons butter or margarine
> 2 cups golden raisins
> ⅛ teaspoon ground nutmeg
> ½ cup firmly packed brown sugar
> ⅔ cup dry white wine
> ½ teaspoon vanilla extract

Powdered Sugar Glaze

> 1½ cups confectioners' sugar
> 1 tablespoon butter or margarine, softened
> ⅛ teaspoon vanilla extract
> 3 tablespoons warm water

1. Sprinkle yeast over the water in large bowl of electric mixer. Add 1 tablespoon of the sugar. Let stand until yeast is soft (about 5 minutes).

2. Add remaining sugar, evaporated milk, salt, and egg.

3. Add 1 cup of the flour. Mix to blend, then beat at medium speed until batter is smooth. Blend in the ¼ cup melted butter.

4. In a large bowl cut the diced butter into the remaining 4 cups flour until particles are about the size of dried peas. Pour yeast batter over mixture; turn carefully with a rubber spatula to blend just until flour is moistened (dough will be very soft).

Cover with plastic wrap and refrigerate for 3 to 5 hours or until next day.

5. Turn dough out onto a floured board or pastry cloth. Press dough into a compact ball and knead briefly just until dough is pliable (6 to 8 turns). Divide dough into two equal portions. Wrap one portion in plastic wrap and return to refrigerator while shaping first half.

6. Roll each half out on a floured surface into a 12- by 16-inch rectangle. Spread with half of the Golden Raisin Filling. Fold in half crosswise to make an 8- by 12-inch rectangle. Cut into 12 strips, each 1 inch wide and 8 inches long. Twist each strip two or three times to make a tight spiral. Pinch open ends together to seal, then place about 2 inches apart on greased baking sheets.

7. Cover shaped rolls lightly with waxed paper and let rise until nearly doubled in bulk (1 to 1½ hours). Preheat oven to 350° F. Brush rolls lightly with egg mixture.

8. Bake until golden brown (20 to 25 minutes). Drizzle warm rolls with Powdered Sugar Glaze. Serve warm or at room temperature.

Makes 2 dozen rolls.

Golden Raisin Filling In a 1½- to 2-quart saucepan combine butter, raisins, nutmeg, sugar, and wine. Bring to a boil over medium-high heat. Cover, reduce heat, and simmer for 10 minutes. Then uncover and cook over medium heat, stirring often, until most of the liquid is gone (about 10 minutes). Remove from heat and stir in vanilla. Let cool completely before spreading over dough.

Powdered Sugar Glaze In a medium bowl combine sugar, butter, and vanilla. Gradually add water, stirring until smooth.

Three delicate sweet rolls: Italian Raisin Braids, Cream Cheese Pinwheels, and Orange Sour-Cream Twists (see pages 80, 81, and opposite for recipes).

TUSCAN VINTAGE BRUNCH

Melon Wedges With Lime

Baked Sausage and Red Pepper Frittata

Sweet-Sour Onions

Green Salad With Creamy Mustard Dressing

Florentine Grape Coffee Cake

Jug White or Red Wine

Caffè Latte

Not all the grapes in Tuscany are pressed for Chianti; they are also strewn over the flat, sweet coffee cake in this Italian-accented brunch. For the best texture, serve the coffee cake immediately after baking. Let the dough rise in the refrigerator overnight, then bake in the morning.

BAKED SAUSAGE AND RED PEPPER FRITTATA

> 1 cup freshly grated Parmesan cheese
> 2 tablespoons each butter or margarine and olive oil
> 1 medium onion, thinly slivered
> 1 sweet red bell pepper, seeded and finely chopped
> 1 clove garlic, minced or pressed
> ¼ cup chopped parsley
> ½ pound Italian sausages
> 12 eggs
> 1 cup milk
> ½ teaspoon salt
> ⅛ teaspoon each ground white pepper and nutmeg
> 2 cups (8 oz) shredded Monterey jack cheese

1. Preheat oven to 325° F. Generously grease a 9- by 13-inch baking dish. Coat sides and bottom evenly with ½ cup of the Parmesan cheese.

2. In a large frying pan melt butter with olive oil over medium heat. Add onion and red pepper; cook, stirring often, until onion is soft and begins to brown. Mix in garlic and parsley, then remove from heat. Spoon onion mixture evenly over bottom of prepared casserole.

3. Remove casings from Italian sausages; crumble into frying pan used to cook onion mixture. Cook, stirring often, until sausage is golden brown. Using a slotted spoon, transfer sausage to casserole with onion mixture.

4. In a large bowl beat together eggs, milk, salt, pepper, and nutmeg. Mix in jack cheese. Pour egg mixture over sausage and vegetables in casserole.

5. Bake, uncovered, for 30 minutes. Sprinkle evenly with the remaining Parmesan cheese. Continue baking until frittata is puffed and golden brown (12 to 15 minutes). Cut into squares or rectangles and serve hot.

Serves 8 to 10.

SWEET-SOUR ONIONS

> 2 pounds (about 6 cups) small white boiling onions
> ⅔ cup red wine vinegar
> ⅓ cup balsamic vinegar
> 1 cup sugar
> ½ teaspoon salt
> 1 cinnamon stick (3 to 4 in.)
> ¼ teaspoon each whole allspice and whole cloves

1. Place unpeeled onions in a large bowl; add boiling water to cover. Let stand for 3 minutes. Drain and cover with cold water until onions are cool to the touch. Peel.

2. In a 3-quart saucepan combine vinegars, sugar, salt, cinnamon stick, allspice, and cloves. Bring to a boil over high heat; boil, uncovered, for 5 minutes. Add onions; adjust heat so mixture boils gently. Cook, uncovered, stirring occasionally, until onions are tender and liquid is syrupy (15 to 20 minutes).

3. Remove onions and a little of the liquid to a serving dish. Serve warm or at room temperature.

Serves 8 to 10.

GREEN SALAD WITH CREAMY MUSTARD DRESSING

> 8 cups torn romaine lettuce
> 4 cups each torn red leaf or butter lettuce and torn spinach leaves
> 2 cups halved cherry tomatoes
> 6 green onions, thinly sliced (use part of tops)
> 1 or 2 jars (6 oz each) marinated artichoke hearts, drained

Creamy Mustard Dressing

> 1 egg yolk
> 2 tablespoons red wine vinegar
> 4 teaspoons Dijon mustard
> 1 clove garlic, minced or pressed
> ½ teaspoon salt
> ⅛ teaspoon pepper
> ⅓ cup each olive oil and salad oil

1. In a large bowl combine greens, cherry tomatoes, and green onions.

2. Just before serving add artichokes. Mix lightly with Creamy Mustard Dressing and serve at once.

Serves 8 to 10.

Creamy Mustard Dressing In a medium bowl mix egg yolk, vinegar, mustard, garlic, salt, and pepper until well combined. Using a whisk or fork, gradually beat in olive oil and salad oil until dressing is thick and creamy.

Makes about 1 cup.

FLORENTINE GRAPE COFFEE CAKE

    1 teaspoon anise seed,
       coarsely crushed
    ½ cup sugar
    1 package active dry yeast
    ¼ cup each warm (105° to
       115° F) water and warm milk
    ⅛ teaspoon salt
    ½ teaspoon vanilla extract
    ½ cup butter or margarine,
       softened
   2½ to 3 cups flour
    1 egg
    3 cups Concord or red
       seedless grapes

1. In a small jar stir together anise seed and sugar; cover and let stand for 8 hours or overnight to blend flavors; pour through a fine sieve to remove seed. Discard seed.

2. Sprinkle yeast over the water in large bowl of electric mixer. Add 1 tablespoon of the anise-flavored sugar. Let stand until yeast is soft (about 5 minutes).

3. Add 2 tablespoons anise sugar, warm milk, salt, vanilla, and butter.

4. Add 1 cup of the flour. Mix to blend, then beat at medium speed until smooth and elastic (about 3 minutes). Beat in egg until smooth. Stir in about 1½ cups more flour to make a soft dough.

5. Turn dough out onto a floured board or pastry cloth. Knead until smooth and satiny and small bubbles form just under surface (5 to 10 minutes), adding just enough flour to prevent dough from being sticky.

6. Turn dough in a greased bowl. Cover with plastic wrap and a towel; let rise in a warm place until doubled in bulk (1¼ to 1½ hours).

7. Punch dough down. Cover with inverted bowl. Let rest for 10 minutes.

8. Roll dough out on a floured surface to a large rectangle. Press into a greased, shallow 10- by 15-inch baking pan. Sprinkle evenly with grapes, then sprinkle grapes with the remaining 5 tablespoons anise sugar.

9. Let rise until dough looks puffy (20 to 25 minutes). Preheat oven to 400° F.

10. Bake coffee cake until well browned (15 to 20 minutes). Let cool slightly, then cut into generous strips.

Makes 1 coffee cake.

CAFFÈ LATTÈ

This Italian coffeehouse favorite is made with hot milk made frothy by steam from an espresso pot with a steam jet—sometimes called a *cappuccino* pot. The only real difference between *caffè lattè* and cappuccino is the size of the cup; cappuccino is served in a smaller one.

    2 cups milk
    2 cups espresso coffee
       Ground cinnamon or
       powdered, sweetened cocoa

1. Using steam from an espresso coffee maker, heat milk in a deep, heatproof container until frothy. Pour most of the milk, reserving a little of the foam, into 4 tall, heatproof mugs.

2. Slowly pour coffee down sides of mugs. Spoon reserved milk foam over coffee. Sprinkle lightly with cinnamon or cocoa.

Makes 4 cups.

DOUGHNUTS AND FRIED BREADS

Freshly made doughnuts and fried breads taste and smell so delicious, it's really a shame so few home bakers seem to make them today. Many of the recipes take no more time than a cake batter or a batch of cookies, and if you've grown up with only the storebought type, you'll find your own far more flavorful and delicate. You can also prepare the dough the day before, so it takes only a few minutes to fry a batch of fresh doughnuts for Sunday breakfast.

For frying you will need a deep kettle of hot fat. Peanut oil or corn oil are better than solid shortening for frying, since the oils can be heated to a higher temperature without smoking. The oil can be used again, but no more than 4 or 5 times. After that it becomes very dark and has an unpleasant odor when heated. After each use, cool the oil completely, strain it through cheesecloth into a bottle, cap tightly, and refrigerate.

The frying vessel can be either a thermostatically controlled electric skillet or deep-fryer, or a small roasting pan or Dutch oven heated on the stove top. Whichever you choose, have 2 to 3 inches of oil in the pan for frying. A pan measuring 9 to 10 inches across will need 2 to 3 quarts of oil.

Keep the frying temperature fairly constant—although it's bound to fluctuate a few degrees while you're cooking. A deep-frying or candy thermometer is your best gauge. Chopsticks or knitting needles are handy tools for turning breads as they fry.

You should wrap and freeze any fried breads you won't use in a day. To reheat, brush off any ice crystals and set on a baking sheet in a 350° F oven for about 7 minutes.

OLD-FASHIONED CAKE DOUGHNUTS

These old favorites are easy and inexpensive to make, with a slightly crunchy outside and a soft, cakelike inside. Serve while still warm.

    1 cup sugar
    4 teaspoons baking powder
    1½ teaspoons salt
    ½ teaspoon ground nutmeg
    2 eggs
    ¼ cup butter, melted
    1 cup milk
    4 to 4½ cups cake flour
      Oil for frying
      Cinnamon Sugar (optional, see page 82)

1. In a large bowl, stir together the sugar, baking powder, salt, and nutmeg to combine.

2. Add eggs, butter, and milk; beat well.

3. Add 3 cups of the flour, beating until thoroughly blended. Add 1 more cup of flour and beat well. The dough should be rather soft, sticky, and just firm enough to handle. If necessary, gradually stir in enough of the remaining flour to make a shaggy-looking, barely manageable mass.

4. Cover with plastic wrap and chill for at least an hour or overnight.

5. Begin heating at least 2 inches of oil to 360° F.

6. Scrape half the chilled dough onto a floured surface, then push, pat, and roll to make a mass about ½ inch thick. Cut doughnuts with a floured doughnut cutter. Set doughnuts and their holes aside on a lightly floured baking sheet. Push the scraps together, reroll, and cut again. Repeat with other half of the dough.

7. Fry about 4 doughnuts and holes at a time: Gently drop them into hot fat, and flip them over as they rise to the surface and puff. Turn a few more times as they cook.

They will take about 2 to 3 minutes and are done when golden brown all over. Remove with a slotted spoon and drain on paper towels. While doughnuts are still warm, toss in Cinnamon Sugar (if used).
Makes about 25 doughnuts and holes.

Chocolate Doughnuts Omit nutmeg. Stir ½ cup unsweetened cocoa with dry ingredients in step 1, and add 1 teaspoon baking soda. Also add 1 teaspoon vanilla extract when you add the milk in step 2.

Whole Wheat Doughnuts Substitute 3½ to 4 cups whole wheat flour for cake flour. These will not be quite as light and delicate.

Spice Doughnuts Add 1½ teaspoons ground cinnamon, 1 teaspoon ground nutmeg, ½ teaspoon ground cloves, and ½ teaspoon ground ginger to the dry ingredients in step 1.

BUÑUELOS

Buñuelos, often available in Mexican bakeries, are small, round, puffy pillows of sweet dough, so light and airy you can hardly stop eating them. Their hollow centers make them perfect for jelly doughnuts.

    ¼ cup butter, softened
    ⅓ cup sugar
    2 eggs
    1 teaspoon vanilla extract
    1¾ cups flour
    2 teaspoons baking powder
    1 teaspoon salt
    ¼ cup milk
      Oil for frying
      Cinnamon Sugar (see page 82)

1. In medium bowl of electric mixer, cream butter and sugar together until blended. Add eggs and beat well. Stir in vanilla.

2. Stir and toss 1 cup of the flour with baking powder and salt. Add to first mixture and mix until blended. Beat in milk. Add the remaining flour and mix to make a soft dough.

3. Turn onto a floured surface and knead a minute or two, until dough is perfectly smooth, kneading in a little more flour if necessary to keep it from being too sticky.

4. Roll dough until it is about ¼ inch thick, flouring it lightly if it sticks. Cut into 3-inch rounds.

5. In a frying kettle, heat about 2 inches of oil to 360° F.

6. Fry about 6 buñuelos at a time, turning them often, for about 1½ to 2 minutes, until they look like puffy, golden pillows. Drain on paper towels and toss in Cinnamon Sugar while still warm.

Makes about 24 buñuelos.

Jelly Buñuelos Fill a pastry bag, fitted with a round tip, with about 2 cups jelly or thick jam. After buñuelos have cooled, use a knife point to make a small slit in the side of each buñuelo. Insert tip of bag and pipe in a generous tablespoon of jam or jelly.

Puffy Buñuelos (opposite page) and cinnamon-sugared Churros (page 90) are enjoyable Mexican doughnuts. Serve them warm with foamy hot chocolate.

89

Choose your favorite from this doughnut array: Old-Fashioned Cake Doughnuts dusted with confectioners' sugar (page 88), sugar-sprinkled Yeast-Raised Doughnuts, plain cake doughnuts, and iced Maple Bars (page 91). Fry the cutouts for bite-sized doughnut holes.

CHURROS

Another Mexican fried bread, *churros* are made with long "ropes" of cream puff paste. They should be eaten warm, when the outside is crisp and golden and the inside so puffy it's almost hollow.

    1 cup water
    ½ teaspoon salt
    1 tablespoon sugar
    ½ cup butter
    1 cup flour
    4 eggs
       Oil for frying
       Cinnamon Sugar (see page 82)

1. Place water, salt, sugar, and butter in a heavy saucepan. Heat slowly until butter melts, then bring to a full boil.

2. Add flour all at once, and beat furiously until the mixture is thick and smooth. Continue beating over medium heat for about 2 minutes, then remove.

3. Add eggs, one at a time, beating vigorously after each until mixture is smooth. (A hand-held electric beater is useful.)

4. Heat about 2 inches of oil to 390° F.

5. Scoop mixture into a large pastry bag fitted with a ½-inch star tip and fold down top of the bag to seal. Squeeze bag over the hot oil, pushing out a rope of paste 4 to 5 inches long. Cut with a knife, letting rope fall gently into oil. Rapidly form about 6 more churros the same way. Turn them frequently until golden, about 2 minutes. Remove with a slotted spoon and drain on paper towels.

6. Fry remaining paste the same way, and while churros are still warm, toss them in Cinnamon Sugar.

Makes 3 to 4 dozen 4- to 5-inch Churros.

Nuns' Sighs As their amusing name implies, nuns' sighs are so light and puffy they are nearly airborne. Rather than making ropes, simply drop heaping tablespoon blobs of paste into hot fat. Fry until golden, turning frequently. Toss in Cinnamon Sugar, arrange on plates, and pour Raspberry Sauce (see below) over each serving.
Makes 2 dozen puffs.

RASPBERRY SAUCE

> 1 box (10 oz) frozen
>   raspberries, thawed
> 2 tablespoons lemon juice,
>   or more to taste

1. Purée the berries and their juice in a blender or food processor. Press through a sieve or strainer to remove seeds.

2. Add lemon juice to taste and refrigerate until needed.

Makes about ¾ cup.

YEAST-RAISED DOUGHNUTS

These doughnuts are softer and lighter than Old-Fashioned Cake Doughnuts (see page 88) because they are leavened with yeast.

> 1 cup warm (105° to 115° F)
>   milk
> 1 package active dry yeast
> ½ cup sugar
> 1½ teaspoons salt
> ¼ teaspoon each *ground
>   cinnamon and nutmeg*
> 2 eggs
> ¼ cup butter, melted
> 3½ to 4 cups flour
>   Oil for frying
>   Cinnamon Sugar (optional,
>   see page 82)

1. Pour the milk in a large mixing bowl, sprinkle on yeast, stir, and let stand a few minutes to dissolve.

2. Add sugar, salt, cinnamon, nutmeg, eggs, and melted butter and beat vigorously until blended.

3. Add 2 cups of the flour and beat until batter is heavy but smooth. Add 1 more cup of flour, beating well, then add enough of the remaining flour to make a soft but manageable dough.

4. Turn out onto a lightly floured surface and knead a few minutes, until dough is smooth and elastic, sprinkling on a little additional flour if necessary to keep it from being too sticky.

5. Place in a greased bowl, cover with plastic wrap, and let rise until doubled in bulk. (Or refrigerate and let rise overnight if you wish to make fresh doughnuts the next morning.)

6. Turn dough out onto a floured surface, punch down, then roll and pat until dough is about ½ inch thick. Cut with a floured doughnut

cutter and set aside on baking sheets covered with waxed paper, leaving about 1½ inches between doughnuts. Reroll scraps and continue until all dough is cut. Cover with a towel and let rise until doubled in bulk.

7. When you are almost ready to fry, heat 2 to 3 inches of oil to 360° F.

8. Gently drop 3 or 4 doughnuts and their holes into hot fat. Turn frequently until golden brown on both sides (about 2 to 3 minutes). Remove with a slotted spoon and drain on paper towels. Fry remaining doughnuts the same way and toss in Cinnamon Sugar (if used) while still warm.

Makes about 18 to 20 doughnuts and holes.

Maple Bars Press, pat, and roll dough to a fairly even rectangle about ½ inch thick. With a sharp knife, trim off any uneven edges. Cut into rectangles about 2 inches wide and 4 inches long. Set aside on baking sheets covered with waxed paper, cover with a towel, and let rise until doubled in bulk. Fry as in Yeast-Raised Doughnuts. While still warm, brush top of each with Maple Glaze (see below).

Makes about 15 bars.

MAPLE GLAZE

> 1 cup confectioners' sugar
> 4 to 5 tablespoons maple syrup

Beat confectioners' sugar and 4 tablespoons of the syrup together until smooth. If glaze is too stiff to spread, beat in a little more syrup.

Makes about ½ cup.

FASTNACHT KIECHLES

Kiechles are German in origin. The name means "fast night cakes," and they were often made before the beginning of the Lenten fast. They are rather sweet and rich in butter, eggs, and fruit.

    1 package active dry yeast
    ½ cup warm (105° to 115° F)
        evaporated milk
    1 egg
    2 egg yolks
    1 teaspoon salt
    ½ cup sugar
    2 teaspoons vanilla extract
        Rind of 1 lemon, grated
    ½ cup butter, melted
    2¾ to 3¼ cups flour
    ½ cup chopped mixed
        candied fruit
    ½ cup dried currants
        Oil for frying
        Cinnamon Sugar (optional,
        see page 82)

1. Stir yeast into warm milk in a large bowl and let stand a few minutes to dissolve.

2. Add egg, egg yolks, salt, sugar, vanilla, lemon rind, and butter and beat until completely mixed.

3. Add 1½ cups of the flour, candied fruit, and currants and beat vigorously until blended. Add enough of the remaining flour to make a soft but manageable dough. Turn out onto a lightly floured surface, knead for 1 to 2 minutes, then stop and let rest for 10 minutes.

4. Resume kneading for about 7 minutes, until the dough is smooth and elastic, sprinkling on a little flour if necessary to keep it from being too sticky. (It's fine if the dough seems a little oily.) Place in a greased bowl, cover, and let rise until doubled in bulk.

5. Punch down dough and turn out onto a lightly floured surface. Roll and pat into a ⅓-inch-thick rectangle about 10 by 13 inches. Cut into smaller rectangles about 1½ by 3 inches and place on a floured baking sheet, leaving room between kiechles for them to rise. Cover with a towel; let rise until doubled in bulk.

6. Heat 2 to 3 inches of oil to 360° F.

7. Fry the kiechles 3 or 4 at a time, turning them often, until golden brown, 2 to 3 minutes. Drain on paper towels and toss in Cinnamon Sugar (if used) while still warm.

Makes about 20 kiechles.

BRIOCHE DOUGH DOUGHNUTS

These deliciously tender and buttery doughnuts melt in the mouth. They are a little richer than the Yeast-Raised Doughnuts.

    Classic Brioche dough,
    completed through step
    5 (see page 94)
    Oil for frying
    Cinnamon Sugar (optional,
    see page 82)

1. Punch risen brioche dough down and turn out onto a lightly floured surface. Push, pat, and roll it until dough is ½ inch thick. Cut with a floured doughnut cutter and set aside on baking sheets covered with waxed paper, leaving about 1½ inches between them. Re-roll scraps and continue until all dough is cut. Cover loosely with a towel and let rise until doubled in bulk.

2. When you are almost ready to fry, heat 2 to 3 inches of oil to 375° F.

3. Gently drop in 3 or 4 doughnuts and their holes and turn frequently until golden brown, about 2 to 3 minutes. Remove with a slotted spoon and drain on paper towels. Fry the remainder the same way and toss in Cinnamon Sugar (if used) while still warm.

Makes about 2 dozen doughnuts and holes.

BEIGNETS

Beignets are sweet, rich rectangular breads, popular in New Orleans at the French Market. Serve them warm, with coffee.

    1 package active dry yeast
    ½ cup warm (105° to 115° F)
        water
    1 egg
    2 tablespoons butter, melted
    ⅓ cup sugar
    1 teaspoon salt
    1 cup evaporated milk
    3¼ to 3½ cups flour
        Oil for frying
        Confectioners' sugar

1. Sprinkle yeast over warm water in a large mixing bowl, stir, and let stand a few minutes to dissolve.

2. Add egg, butter, sugar, salt, and evaporated milk and mix well.

3. Add 2 cups of flour and beat vigorously until blended. Gradually add enough remaining flour to make a manageable dough.

4. Knead on a floured surface for several minutes, until dough is smooth, then place in a greased bowl, cover with plastic wrap, and let rise overnight in refrigerator.

5. Roll chilled dough on a floured surface to a ¼-inch-thick rectangle about 12 by 24 inches. With a long, sharp knife, cut into squares about 2 or 3 inches to a side. Cover with a towel and let rest for about 20 minutes.

6. In the meantime, heat about 1½ inches of oil to 360° F.

7. Fry 4 or 5 beignets at a time, turning them frequently, for 2 to 3 minutes, until they are puffy and brown. Drain on paper towels, then sprinkle with confectioners' sugar and serve.

Makes about 30 beignets.

BRIOCHE

Of all the breakfast breads in this section, brioche is probably the easiest to make. You'll probably find it no more difficult to make than a loaf of plain white bread. If you have a powerful food processor, the mixing and kneading take just a few minutes, and after the dough has had its first rise, you can punch it down and refrigerate it for up to a few days before forming and baking if you wish. So like all breads, it can be made to suit your schedule.

Brioche is so satisfying, its flavor so buttery, and its texture so creamy that it is perfect for a light breakfast. Individual brioches, with their wide, ridged base and a tiny, slightly lopsided topknot, are baked in small, fluted molds about 1 inch high and 3 inches across at the top, tapering down to about 1½ inches at the bottom. If you don't have molds, you can use muffin tins, but they don't have the traditional ridged bottom. Baked in a rectangular bread pan, a thinly sliced brioche loaf makes good tea sandwiches, toast, or bread pudding. Brioche goes stale quickly, so freeze what you won't use in a day or two.

Bake Classic Brioche (page 94) in a loaf pan to serve with café au lait *for a Continental breakfast. This brioche was formed into three parts, in the style of Normandy bakers.*

93

CLASSIC BRIOCHE

Here is a good brioche: It is fine-textured, light, and tastes of butter and eggs. It can be baked as a loaf or in the small brioche molds. After its first rising, you can also use this dough to make delicious raised doughnuts (see page 92).

The method below is for hand-mixed dough; instructions for using the food processor appear afterward.

> 1 package active dry yeast
> 2 tablespoons sugar
> ½ cup warm (105° to 115° F) milk
> 1½ teaspoons salt
> 2 eggs
> 2 egg yolks
> 3¼ to 3½ cups flour
> 12 tablespoons butter (softened if mixing by hand, chilled otherwise)
> 1 egg mixed with 2 teaspoons water, for glaze

To Mix by Hand

1. Sprinkle yeast and sugar over warm milk in a large bowl, stir, and let stand a few minutes to dissolve.

2. Add salt, eggs, and egg yolks and mix well.

3. Add 2 cups of the flour and beat vigorously until batter is smooth and heavy. Drop in softened butter, a tablespoon at a time, and beat after each addition until incorporated. If some tiny lumps of butter remain, don't worry; they will blend in later.

4. Add 1 cup of the remaining flour and mix well until a rough mass forms, then scrape out onto a lightly floured surface. Knead for a couple of minutes, sprinkling on a little more flour as necessary to keep dough from being too sticky. Stop kneading and let rest for about 5 to 10 minutes. Continue kneading for a few minutes more, until dough is smooth and elastic.

5. Place in a greased bowl, cover, and let rise until dough is puffy and slightly more than doubled in bulk (about 1 hour).

6. Punch dough down. Cover and refrigerate for a day or two at this point, if desired. (The dough will continue to rise until it is thoroughly chilled; just punch it down every hour or so.) To form the dough now, continue below to make individual brioches, or see step 9 to make a loaf.

7. Cut dough in half and on a lightly floured surface shape each piece into an even rope about 10 inches long. Cut each rope into 7 pieces, each about 1½ inches long. Plump each piece of dough into a smooth ball by holding it in one hand as you tuck the edges underneath with the fingers of your other hand, thus forming a tight round with a seam on the bottom. Cover with a towel and let rest for 10 minutes.

8. *To form brioches:* Generously butter 14 brioche molds or muffin tins. Pick up a piece of dough and pinch it with your fingertips, gently stretching the ball to elongate it slightly as you pull away a marble-sized piece of dough—but don't detach it completely. To form the topknot, place the dough on floured surface, lay your index finger on top of the stretch, then roll your finger back and forth, to stretch the small end of dough out about another inch. Twist the topknot three or four times and press it firmly back into the larger base. The shape resembles a tiny snowman with a fat body and a tiny head. Place in one of the prepared molds, pressing down firmly around the edges. Form the remaining balls the same way. Place all the filled molds on a baking sheet, cover loosely with a towel, and let rise until a little more than doubled in bulk and puffed well over the tops of the molds. Continue with step 10.

9. *To form a loaf:* Butter a 9- by 5-inch loaf pan. Form dough into a smooth loaf and place it in pan. Cover and let rise until doubled in bulk (about 1 hour). After rising, use a sharp, pointed knife to make a ½-inch-deep slash lengthwise down the center.

10. Preheat oven to 375° F. Before baking, paint the tops of each brioche (or the loaf) with egg glaze, taking care not to let it run down into the molds.

11. Bake small brioches (on a baking sheet) for about 20 minutes, turning pan once or twice during baking if they brown unevenly. Bake loaf for about 50 minutes; if it browns too much, cover loosely with a tent of foil for the remainder of the baking time.

12. Remove from oven and turn out onto racks (if any stick, pry them out with a knife point) to cool completely before wrapping for storage or freezing.

13. To reheat, place on a baking sheet in a 350° F oven for about 10 minutes.

Makes 14 three-inch brioches, or 1 loaf.

To Mix with a Processor

1. Sprinkle yeast and sugar over warm milk in a small bowl, stir, and let stand a few minutes to dissolve.

2. Pour yeast mixture into bowl of a food processor fitted with steel blade. Add salt, eggs, and egg yolks and whirl for a few seconds.

3. Add 2 cups of the flour and process again until smooth. While blade is turning, drop in chilled butter in 2-tablespoon chunks. Continue to process until smooth.

4. Add another 1½ cups of the flour. Process again until dough comes together and forms a rough ball that revolves around the bowl; process for 30 seconds more. Continue with step 5 of the preceding recipe for the rising and forming. (Some food processors tend to strain while kneading a dough. If yours labors or stalls, remove dough and continue kneading by hand.)

BRIOCHE BATTER BREAD

This is not as firm and fine-textured as a loaf made from the classic brioche dough, but it's easy and fast to mix up in an electric mixer or processor, and it makes good tea sandwiches and toast. Lacking machinery, beat the batter with a big wooden spoon or your bare hand.

> 1 package active dry yeast
> ½ cup warm (105° to 115° F) milk
> 10 tablespoons butter, melted and cooled slightly
> 3 eggs
> 1 tablespoon sugar
> 1 teaspoon salt
> 2 cups flour
> 1 egg mixed with 2 teaspoons water, for glaze

1. In large bowl of electric mixer, sprinkle yeast over warm milk, stir, and let stand a few minutes to dissolve. (If you are using a food processor, dissolve yeast in a small bowl, then pour it into work bowl fitted with steel blade.)

2. Add butter, eggs, sugar, and salt and beat until completely mixed, or whirl for several seconds in the processor.

3. Add 1 cup of the flour and mix vigorously until smooth. Dump in remaining flour and beat like fury until batter is smooth and heavy. In the processor, whirl until completely blended and smooth, then scrape the batter into a bowl. Cover with plastic wrap and let rise until doubled in bulk.

4. Beat batter well, then scoop it into a buttered by 4½- by 8½-inch loaf pan. It's sticky, so use wet fingertips to press it into the corners and smooth the top. Cover loosely with a towel and let rise until edges of batter are ½ to 1 inch from the top of the pan (about 1 hour).

5. Preheat oven to 375° F. Brush top of risen loaf with egg glaze and make a ½-inch-deep gash down the center with a sharp, pointed knife. Bake until bread is well browned and has shrunk just a hairline from the sides of the pan (about 45 minutes). If it begins to brown too much, cover loosely with a tent of foil.

6. Let cool in pan for about 10 minutes, then turn out onto a rack to cool completely before slicing.

Makes 1 loaf.

Four stages of individual brioches: balls of dough; dough elongated to form topknots; unbaked brioches with topknots in place; and baked brioches.

Flaky Croissants (recipe opposite) are shaped from triangles of butter-flecked dough, rolled from the wide end toward the point, then curved into a crescent.

CROISSANTS

Buttery, flaky croissants are not beyond the scope of any good home baker. Though the recipe requires frequent attention during the first couple of hours, after that you are free to continue in stages—finishing the croissants in the next day or two if you wish.

The success of croissant dough (and of Danish pastry dough) depends very much on temperature: The dough must have frequent chillings in the refrigerator. Cooling makes the dough easier to roll out during the repeated rollings and foldings, or "turns."

With each turn, you are in a sense laminating dozens of layers of yeast dough with layers of butter (much like making puff pastry), which will rise and then puff into thin, flaky layers in the oven. Chilling keeps the dough from becoming soft, oily, and hard to handle. Also choose a cool day or work in an air-conditioned kitchen; this isn't a project for a humid summer afternoon.

Whether you use salted or unsalted butter in your croissants is a matter of taste.

CROISSANTS

With so many steps, croissant making might seem like quite a difficult task at first glance—but it's really not hard, just perhaps a bit time-consuming. The technique of building thin layers of butter between layers of yeast dough will be familiar if you have ever made puff pastry, and even if you haven't, instructions are detailed enough for beginning bakers. Follow directions carefully and you should have no trouble producing the lightest, flakiest croissants you've ever had.

Yeast Dough

1 package active dry yeast
1¼ cups warm (105° to 115° F) milk
2 teaspoons sugar
1½ teaspoons salt
2¾ cups flour

Butter Mixture

1¼ cups cold butter
3 tablespoons flour

Egg Glaze

1 egg mixed with 1 teaspoon water

1. *To prepare yeast dough:* Sprinkle yeast over the warm milk in a large bowl, add sugar, stir, and let stand for a few minutes to dissolve. Add salt and flour, then mix vigorously but briefly, just until you have a rough, sticky dough that holds together. Set aside for about 5 minutes while you prepare the butter mixture.

2. *To prepare butter mixture:* Cut the butter into tablespoon-sized bits, dropping them onto your work surface, then sprinkling with flour. Tear off two good-sized sheets of waxed paper and set aside. Begin mashing butter and flour together by smearing across work surface with the heel of your hand; gather mixture into a pile with a spatula or pastry scraper, then repeat smearing a couple of times—until butter is smooth and workable, but

still cold. Flour your hands, then form butter into a small, rough rectangle and place it between sheets of waxed paper. Roll and pat butter into a larger rectangle 6 by 8 inches, keeping sides as even as possible. Set aside while you roll out yeast dough.

3. Wipe work surface clean, sprinkle it generously with flour, and turn dough out onto it. Flour the dough, which is quite soft, and push, pat, and roll it into a rectangle about 10 by 14 inches. Unwrap butter and place it on bottom half of dough, leaving about a 1-inch border on 3 sides. Lift up the top of the dough, working it loose with a spatula or scraper if it sticks to work surface, and flip it over the butter. Pinch edges to seal. Give the dough a quarter turn, so sealed flap is to your right.

4. Using smooth, even strokes, roll to a rectangle 9 by 17 inches. Check to see if it is sticking and sprinkle with flour if necessary—don't be afraid to pick it up and look. Fold bottom third of dough up over the middle, then flip top third down to cover it. Turn again so flap is to your right and roll out again to 9 by 17 inches. Fold in thirds as before, flour lightly, wrap in plastic wrap, place in a plastic bag, and chill for about 30 minutes. At this point, the first two turns are finished.

5. Roll chilled dough again to 9 by 17 inches, fold in thirds, wrap in plastic wrap and a plastic bag, and refrigerate for 45 minutes. (If at any time dough becomes soft and resists rolling out, or if butter breaks through in large, smeary patches, stop working, dust dough with flour, then slide onto a baking sheet and chill for about 20 minutes.)

6. Roll out and fold dough again, thus completing four turns. Wrap and chill for at least 1 hour (or for a few hours or overnight if it's more convenient) before forming croissants.

7. Roll dough out to 10 by 20 inches, keeping sides as even as possible. With a sharp knife, cut in half lengthwise, then cut each half into four 5-inch squares. Cut each square in half diagonally, to make 2 triangles.

8. Working with one triangle at a time, pick up the two closest points, at the base, and gently stretch them out to about 7 inches. Hold these two points down with one hand and use the other hand to wiggle and stretch the other, farthest point out to about 7 inches or more. Starting at the base, roll up stretched dough just like a crescent roll. Pull points down, toward one another, to form a crescent shape.

9. Place the croissants on baking sheets, leaving 2 inches between each one. Cover with a towel and let rise for about 1½ hours, or more, until puffy and doubled in size. (If you've used two baking sheets and your oven can hold only one sheet on the same rack, chill one sheet for the first hour or so, to slow rising, so baking times are staggered.)

10. Preheat oven to 425° F and place a rack in middle level. Brush each risen croissant with egg glaze and bake for about 12 to 15 minutes, until well browned and puffy. If they are not browning evenly, quickly turn pan around from front to back once or twice during baking. If some are done before others, just remove them with a spatula. Transfer croissants to a rack to cool for a few minutes before serving. Wrap and freeze what you won't use in a day. (To reheat, unwrap and set on a baking sheet, still frozen, and place in a 400° F oven for about 7 minutes.)

Makes 16 four-inch croissants.

Danish Pastry, the flakiest and most buttery of all sweet rolls, is ethereal baked as Cinnamon Rolled Danish (page 102).

DANISH PASTRIES

With a little time and patience, you can easily turn out fancy Danish pastries that are better than those you see in the best bakeries in town. At home you can be certain of using real butter, and you can shape the pastries any way you wish and fill them with your own freshly made fillings. And you will have them all for a fraction of the cost of those you buy. Since Danish dough is made just like croissant dough, the important points that apply to croissant making apply here also. Keep the dough chilled as recommended through the recipe and work on a cool day or in an air-conditioned kitchen; the dough will be much easier to handle.

It is best to spread this project over two or three days by making the fillings one day, the dough the next, then forming and baking on the third day. It's a good idea to divide the work up, especially if you are new to this type of baking. To complete the entire project in a single day would be quite a commitment.

You can use salted butter to make Danish pastries as well as croissants, but you can use unsalted butter if you prefer, with no difference in the taste.

DANISH PASTRY DOUGH

Danish pastry dough is slightly richer than croissant dough because it contains eggs and a little more sugar.

Yeast Dough

  2 packages active dry yeast
  1 cup warm (105° to 115°F) milk
  2 eggs, at room temperature
  2 teaspoons salt
  ¼ cup sugar
  3¼ cups flour

Butter Mixture

  1½ cups cold butter
  ¼ cup flour

1. *To prepare yeast dough:* Sprinkle yeast over warm milk in a large bowl, stir, and let stand a few minutes to dissolve. Add eggs, salt, and sugar and mix well. Dump in flour and mix briefly, just until you have a rough, sticky dough that holds together. Set aside for about 5 minutes while you prepare butter mixture.

2. *To prepare butter mixture:* Cut butter into tablespoon-sized chunks, dropping them onto your work surface. Sprinkle with flour. Mix butter and flour together by smearing them out in front of you with the heel of your hand; gather up the mixture and smear again three or four times until butter is perfectly smooth and workable but still cold. Flour your hands and pat mixture into a rectangle about 4 by 5 inches. Place between two sheets of waxed paper and pat and roll into a larger rectangle 7 by 9 inches, keeping edges as even as possible. Set aside for a moment.

3. Scrape surface clean, sprinkle it generously with flour, and turn yeast dough out onto it—it will be quite soft. Sprinkle top of dough with flour, then roll and pat into a 10- by 14-inch rectangle. Unwrap butter and set it on bottom half of dough, leaving a 1-inch border on three sides. Gently lift up unbuttered top flap and flip it down over butter. Pinch the edges to seal, then use a wide spatula or scraper to help lift dough package and give it a quarter turn, so the sealed flap is to your right.

4. *To roll out and fold dough:* Follow steps 4, 5, and 6 of Croissants (see page 97), except that you roll out Danish dough a little larger, to an 8- by 20-inch rectangle, since you are working with more dough. After you've completed all the turns, you are ready to form and bake the pastries—or if it is more convenient, wrap dough in plastic wrap and a plastic bag, and refrigerate overnight before forming and baking.

Makes about 2 dozen or more pastries, depending on shapes.

FORMING AND BAKING DANISH

The dough recipe on this page makes about two dozen pastries, and each shape described on the next page requires half the dough. It's fun to make two different shapes and at least two fillings— the more variety, the more professional your pastries will look. After you cut the dough in half, wrap and chill the piece you are not working on.

You can make fillings a day ahead (see pages 102–103), since they all keep well if covered and refrigerated (or frozen). Use the leftovers as cake or cookie fillings, and serve fillings made with fruit with ice cream or puddings.

If you need to use two baking sheets when you bake the Danish and can't fit both pans on the same oven rack, refrigerate one batch after forming and let the other rise at room temperature. The chilled batch will rise more slowly so that baking times will be staggered.

If you're going to freeze Danish, omit any icing called for after baking. Ice the pastries after reheating them in a 400°F oven for about 5 minutes and they'll look freshly made.

HOW TO MAKE DANISH SHAPES

These photographs show you basic Danish pastry shapes.

Corkscrews *Corkscrews, which are very easy to twist into shape, are the fastest Danish pastries to make since they require no special filling.*

Filled Crescents *Although formed like croissants, these crescents have a sweet filling. To make them savory, substitute ham or crumbled bacon, if you wish.*

Open Packets *Open packets are a nice way to show off a variety of fillings, and they eliminate the guesswork when choosing the pastry you want!*

Bear Claws *Bear claws, with their curved shape and toothlike edges, are also known as cockscombs because they resemble a rooster's comb.*

Pinwheels *Pinwheels seem to be a favorite with everyone, perhaps because they vaguely look like the old-fashioned toy of the same name.*

Turnovers *Turnovers are like sealed envelopes enclosing a surprise you discover at the first bite. Seal them well so that they don't unfold when baked.*

Cinnamon Rolled Danish *These puff up in the center when baked to resemble the coiled shell of a snail and are therefore often called snails.*

CORKSCREWS

- ½ recipe Danish Pastry Dough (see page 99)
- 1 egg beaten with 1 teaspoon water
- ⅔ cup Cinnamon Sugar (see page 82)

1. Roll dough on a lightly floured surface into a 15-inch square. Brush dough with some of the beaten egg. Sprinkle evenly with Cinnamon Sugar, pressing it into dough with your fingers.

2. Cut square in half, then cut each half into 10 strips, about 1½ inches wide. Pick up each strip and twist it several times to form a long spiral. Pinch each end firmly, and place strips about 1 inch apart on a baking sheet. (If some of the sugar falls off during the forming, don't worry; it's bound to happen.) Cover with a towel and let rise until almost doubled in bulk (about 45 minutes or slightly longer). Brush each with some of the remaining egg.

3. Preheat oven to 400° F. Bake until golden brown and puffy (about 12 minutes). Transfer to racks to cool.

Makes 20 corkscrews.

FILLED CRESCENTS

- ½ recipe Danish Pastry Dough (see page 99)
- 1 cup Nut, Fig, Prune, or Date Filling (see pages 102–103)
- 1 egg beaten with 1 teaspoon water

1. Roll dough on a lightly floured surface into a rectangle 10 by 15 inches. Cut into six 5-inch squares, then cut each square in half diagonally, to make triangles.

2. Spread 1 generous tablespoon of filling along base or short side of each triangle. Stretch each point of the triangle out slightly; then, beginning from edge with filling, roll up each triangle. Pull ends down slightly to form a crescent shape and place 2 inches apart on a baking sheet. (For more detailed explanation of stretching out points and forming crescents, see Croissants, page 97.) Cover with a towel and let rise until about doubled in bulk (45 minutes to an hour). Brush each crescent with beaten egg.

3. Preheat oven to 400° F. Bake until puffy and golden (12 to 14 minutes). Transfer to racks to cool.

Makes 1 dozen crescents.

OPEN PACKETS

½ recipe Danish Pastry Dough (see page 99)
1 cup Cheese, Apricot, Peach, Apple, Prune, or Nut Filling (see pages 102–103)
1 egg beaten with 1 teaspoon water
Icing (see page 103)
¼ cup slivered almonds

1. Roll dough on a lightly floured surface into a rectangle 12 by 16 inches. Cut lengthwise into three 4-inch strips, then cut each strip into four 4-inch squares.

2. Place about 1½ tablespoons of filling in center of each square. Gently pull on 2 diagonally opposite corners to stretch squares out a bit, then fold them over to the center so they overlap slightly on top of filling. Rub the joined points with drops of beaten egg and pinch them together so they stick. Place about 2 inches apart on baking sheets, cover with a towel, and let rise until nearly doubled in bulk (about 45 minutes to 1 hour). Brush with beaten egg.

3. Preheat oven to 400° F. Bake until puffy and golden (12 to 14 minutes). Transfer to racks to cool, and while still warm brush each with Icing and sprinkle with a few almonds.

Makes 12 packets.

TURNOVERS

½ recipe Danish Pastry Dough (page 99)
1 egg beaten with 1 teaspoon water
1 cup Prune, Date, Apricot, or Apple Filling (see pages 102–103)
Icing (see page 103)

1. Roll dough on a lightly floured surface into a rectangle 12 by 16 inches. Cut lengthwise into 3 strips, 4 by 16 inches, then cut each strip into four 4-inch squares.

2. Brush the edges of each square with some of the beaten egg, then place a generous tablespoon of the filling in the center of each. Fold the squares in half diagonally, to make triangular-shaped turnovers, and press the edges firmly with your fingers to seal. Place about 2 inches apart on baking sheets, cover with a towel, and let rise until puffy and nearly doubled in bulk (about 45 minutes). Brush with some of the beaten egg.

3. Preheat oven to 400° F. Bake until golden brown and puffy (about 12 to 15 minutes).

4. Transfer to racks to cool and brush each with Icing while still warm.

Makes 1 dozen turnovers.

BEAR CLAWS

½ recipe Danish Pastry Dough (page 99)
1 egg beaten with 1 teaspoon water
1 cup Date, Poppy Seed, or Nut Filling (see pages 102–103)
Icing (see page 103)

1. Roll dough on a lightly floured surface into a rectangle 12 by 16 inches. Cut lengthwise into 3 strips, 4 by 16 inches, then cut each strip into four 4-inch squares.

2. Brush edges of each square with some egg mixture. Place about 1 tablespoon of filling in the center of each, spreading it slightly down toward bottom and across center. Fold top half of dough down to cover filling and press edges firmly to seal. Make about seven ½-inch cuts at long, sealed edge of each rectangle, spacing cuts about ½ inch apart. Gently bend each rectangle into a curve, so cuts open slightly, forming claws. Place about 2 inches apart on baking sheets. Cover with a towel and let rise until almost doubled in bulk (about 45 minutes or a little longer). Brush each pastry with some of the remaining egg.

3. Preheat oven to 400° F. Bake until puffy and well browned (about 12 to 14 minutes). Transfer the bear claws to racks to cool and brush each with a little Icing while still warm.

Makes 1 dozen bear claws.

Pain au Chocolat Omit the filling. Finely chop 6 ounces semisweet chocolate. After brushing the edges of the squares with the beaten egg, sprinkle the center of each with a tablespoon of the chopped chocolate. Fold over and pinch the edges to seal but do not make any cuts—these should be rectangular. Let rise; bake and ice as directed for Bear Claws.

CINNAMON ROLLED DANISH

½ cup dried currants
½ recipe Danish Pastry Dough
 (see page 99)
4 tablespoons melted butter
½ cup Cinnamon Sugar (see
 page 82)
½ cup chopped walnuts
 or pecans
1 egg beaten with 1
 teaspoon water
 Icing (see page 103)

1. Pour boiling water over the currants in a small bowl and set aside while you roll out dough.

2. Roll dough on a floured surface into a rectangle 11 by 17 inches. Brush with melted butter, then sprinkle evenly with Cinnamon Sugar. Sprinkle on nuts. Drain currants and pat them dry with paper towels, then distribute them over dough. Press ingredients into the dough with your fingertips. Starting with a long side, roll into a tight cylinder, like a jelly roll. Cut into 1-inch slices and place about 2 inches apart on baking sheets. Cover with a towel and let rise until puffy and almost doubled in bulk (about 45 minutes to 1 hour). Brush each slice with some of the beaten egg.

3. Preheat oven to 400° F. Bake until well browned (about 12 to 14 minutes). Transfer to wire racks to cool; brush with Icing while still warm.

Makes about 18 rolls.

Muffin Puffs Roll dough into a cylinder and cut into rounds as directed above. Place each round in a well-buttered muffin tin, pressing it down with your fingers. Cover and let rise until dough about doubles in bulk and rises well over the tops of tins. Brush with beaten egg and bake until golden brown and puffed even more (about 15 minutes). Cool for 2 to 3 minutes in the pans, then ease out onto racks.

Poppy Seed Rolls Omit Cinnamon Sugar and chopped nuts and instead spread dough with a double recipe of Poppy Seed Filling (see below) before rolling and forming.

Coffee Cake Ring After filling and rolling up dough as directed, form into a large circle by bringing the two ends together. Overlap them slightly, brush with some of the egg mixture, and press them firmly to make as neat and tight a seal as you can. With scissors, make several deep, slanting cuts all around, spacing them about 1 inch apart and cutting to within about ½ inch of bottom of ring. Pull and turn out cuts all around to expose the spiral interior. Lift onto a baking sheet, cover, and let rise until doubled in bulk (1 to 1½ hours). Brush with egg mixture and bake for about 25 minutes, until well browned. Slide into a rack to cool and drizzle with Icing while still warm.

Makes 1 ten-inch ring.

PINWHEELS

½ recipe Danish Pastry Dough
 (see page 99)
1 cup Prune, Nut, or Apple
 Filling (see recipes at right
 and page 103)
1 egg beaten with 1
 teaspoon water
 Icing (see page 103)

1. Roll dough on a lightly floured surface into a rectangle 12 by 16 inches. Cut lengthwise into 3 strips, 4 by 16 inches, then cut each strip into four 4-inch squares.

2. Separate squares. With a small, sharp knife, make diagonal cuts at corners of each, cutting in from corner to about ½ inch from center.

Place a generous tablespoon of filling in middle of each. One by one, fold over alternating points from edge to center, overlapping them a bit. Wet overlapping points with drops of egg mixture, then pinch firmly together with your fingers so they stick. Place about 2 inches apart on baking sheets, cover with a towel, and let rise until almost doubled in bulk (about 45 minutes to 1 hour). Brush with some of the beaten egg.

3. Preheat oven to 400° F. Bake until puffy and golden brown (about 12 to 14 minutes). Transfer to racks to cool and brush each with Icing while still warm.

Makes 1 dozen pinwheels.

PRUNE FILLING

1 cup (8 oz) finely cut
 pitted prunes
⅓ cup water
¼ cup brown sugar
1 tablespoon lemon juice

In a small, heavy-bottomed saucepan, combine prunes, water, and sugar. Simmer gently for several minutes, stirring frequently, until mass is thick enough to hold its shape and prunes have absorbed the water. Stir in lemon juice.

Makes about 1½ cups.

POPPY SEED FILLING

½ cup poppy seed
1 egg
1 egg white
5 tablespoons confectioners'
 sugar
¼ dry bread crumbs

Combine poppy seed, egg, egg white, confectioners' sugar, and bread crumbs and mix until thoroughly combined. Set aside for 20 minutes or so before using.

Makes about ¾ cup.

APRICOT FILLING

1 cup (6 oz) finely chopped
  dried apricots
3 tablespoons sugar
¼ cup chopped almonds

Put apricots in a small saucepan, cover them with water, and simmer over moderate heat until tender. Drain thoroughly. Purée in a food processor or pass through a food mill, then beat in sugar and almonds.

Makes about 1¼ cups.

Peach Filling Substitute 1 cup (6 oz) coarsely chopped dried peaches for the apricots.

APPLE FILLING

4 medium-sized apples
⅓ cup sugar
2 tablespoons dried currants
2 tablespoons chopped walnuts
1 teaspoon lemon juice

Peel and core apples then shred them on the coarse side of a grater. Add the sugar, currants, walnuts, and lemon juice and blend thoroughly.

Makes about 1½ cups.

NUT FILLING

1 cup walnuts, hazelnuts,
  or almonds
¼ cup sugar
1 egg white
1 tablespoon butter, softened

Chop nuts into very fine pieces—about ⅛ inch, or about the size of coarse bread crumbs. A food processor works well. Add the sugar, egg white, and butter and beat until blended.

Makes about ¾ cup.

DATE FILLING

1 cup (8 oz) finely cut
  pitted dates
½ cup water
¼ cup brown sugar
2 teaspoons grated orange rind

In a small, heavy saucepan, combine dates, water, brown sugar, and orange rind. Cook over low heat, stirring frequently, until mixture is thick enough to hold its shape and dates have absorbed the water.

Makes about 1½ cups.

Fig Filling Substitute 1 cup (8 oz) finely cut dried figs for the dates and reduce the sugar to 2 tablespoons.

CHEESE FILLING

1 cup cottage cheese
2 tablespoons sugar
3 tablespoons flour
1 egg yolk
2 teaspoons grated orange rind
¼ cup dried currants (optional)

Press cottage cheese through a strainer or food mill two or three times, until it is fairly smooth, or simply whirl for several seconds in a food processor. Add the sugar, flour, egg yolk, orange rind, and currants (if used) and mix thoroughly.

Makes about 1¼ cups.

ICING

1½ cups confectioners' sugar
3 tablespoons water
¼ teaspoon vanilla extract

In a small bowl, mix confectioners' sugar, water, and vanilla; blend well until icing is thick, smooth, and slightly runny.

Makes about ¾ cup.

HOW TO MAKE FILLED DANISH

The amount of filling used in each Danish may not look generous, but it's better to have too little than too much, which would bubble up and leak out during baking.

Be sure to press very firmly when sealing the edges of unbaked pastries, using your fingertips or the tines of a fork so that the pastries don't pop open in the oven. No matter how well you seal, they may come undone once in a while, but not to worry—it happens to even the best of bakers.

Some bakers prefer fillings simply flavored and not too sweet, but you can add a little more sugar if you wish or spice them up with cinnamon, nutmeg, or cloves.

TREASURED HOLIDAY BREADS

Breads play an important part in the observance of major holidays around the world. An entire cookbook could probably be written if all of them were to be included. Flour millers say that in our culture Easter and Christmas are the occasions for most such baking.

HOT CROSS BUNS

One of the signs that Easter is approaching is the appearance in bakery windows of fruit-studded, icing-crowned hot cross buns. But they are never better than the ones you bake at home. If you make them ahead and freeze them, wait until shortly before serving to apply the frosting crosses.

  2 *packages active dry yeast*
  ½ *cup warm (105 to 115° F)*
     water
  ½ *cup sugar*
  1 *cup warm (105 to 115° F)*
     milk
  1 *teaspoon salt*
  ½ *teaspoon ground nutmeg*
  ¼ *cup butter or margarine,*
     softened
  6 *to 6½ cups flour*
  4 *eggs*
  ½ *cup dried currants*
  ⅔ *cup diced mixed candied fruits*

White Icing

  1½ *cups confectioners' sugar*
  ¼ *teaspoon vanilla extract*
  2 *to 2½ tablespoons warm milk*

1. Sprinkle yeast over the warm water in large bowl of electric mixer. Add 1 tablespoon of the sugar. Let stand until yeast is soft (about 5 minutes).

2. Add remaining sugar, warm milk, salt, nutmeg, and butter.

3. Add 3 cups of the flour. Mix to blend, then beat at medium speed until smooth and elastic (about 5 minutes). Separate one of the eggs; reserve white for glazing buns. Beat yolk and remaining 3 eggs, one at a time, into batter, beating until smooth after each addition.

4. Stir in currants and candied fruits, then mix in about 2½ cups more flour to make a soft dough.

5. Turn dough out onto a board or pastry cloth coated with some of the remaining ½ to 1 cup flour. Knead until dough is smooth and satiny and small bubbles form just under surface (15 to 20 minutes), adding just enough flour to prevent dough from being sticky.

6. Turn dough in a greased bowl. Cover with plastic wrap and a towel; let rise in a warm place until doubled in bulk (1 to 1½ hours).

7. Punch dough down. Cover with inverted bowl and let rest for about 10 minutes.

8. Divide dough into 24 equal portions. Roll each into a smooth ball. Place about 1½ inches apart on greased baking sheets.

9. Let rolls rise until almost doubled in bulk (25 to 30 minutes). Preheat oven to 375° F.

10. Beat reserved egg white slightly with 1 teaspoon water. Brush lightly over rolls. Using a floured razor blade, make ½-inch-deep crisscross slashes in top of each roll.

11. Bake until rolls are richly browned (20 to 25 minutes). Transfer to wire racks to cool. Pipe an icing cross on top of each roll.

Makes 2 dozen rolls.

White Icing Combine sugar and vanilla. Beat in milk, adding it gradually, just until icing is smooth and of a good consistency for piping.

LUCIA BUNS

Swedish bakers can't wait to begin their December holiday baking— these inventively shaped, cardamom-spiced rolls are fashioned for December 13, Saint Lucia Day. But their flavor is just right for Christmas, too.

  2 *packages active dry yeast*
  ½ *cup warm (105 to 115° F)*
     water
  1¼ *cups warm (105 to 115° F)*
     milk
  ½ *cup butter or margarine,*
     softened
  ¾ *cup sugar*
  1 *teaspoon each salt and*
     ground cardamom
  2 *tablespoons grated*
     orange rind
  6 *to 6½ cups flour*
  2 *eggs*
  ½ *cup dried currants*
     Raisins and halved candied
     cherries
  1 *egg white, beaten with 1*
     teaspoon water
     Coarse granulated sugar or
     crushed sugar cubes

1. Sprinkle yeast over the warm water in large bowl of electric mixer. Let stand until soft (about 5 minutes).

2. Stir in milk, butter, sugar, salt, cardamom, and orange rind, stirring until sugar dissolves. Add 3½ cups of the flour. Mix to blend, then beat at medium speed until smooth and elastic (about 5 minutes).

3. Beat in eggs, one at a time, beating until smooth after each addition. Mix in currants. Gradually stir in about 2 cups more flour to make a soft dough.

4. Turn dough out onto a board or pastry cloth coated with some of the remaining ½ to 1 cup flour. Knead until dough is smooth and satiny and small bubbles form just under surface (12 to 15 minutes). Add enough flour to keep dough from being sticky.

5. Turn dough in a greased bowl. Cover with plastic wrap and a towel; let rise in a warm place until doubled in bulk (1 to 1½ hours).

6. Punch dough down; turn out on a floured surface, cover with inverted bowl, and let rest for 10 minutes. Divide dough into two equal portions. Roll each into a 12-inch square. Cut each square in half to make two 6-by 12-inch rectangles. Cut each rectangle crosswise into 12 strips. Roll each strip into a pencil-thin strand 8 inches long.

7. On greased baking sheets cross two strands to make an X. Curl each end into a small coil. Place a raisin in center of half the coils; place a cherry half in remaining coils. Repeat until all dough is shaped into rolls. Brush rolls lightly with egg white mixture. Sprinkle with coarse sugar. Let rise until almost doubled (30 to 40 minutes). Preheat oven to 400° F.

8. Bake rolls until golden brown (12 to 15 minutes). Serve warm or at room temperature.

Makes 2 dozen rolls.

CHRISTMAS PANETTONE

In Italy *panettone* means Christmas. Legend has it that this Milanese bread, baked from a golden brioche-like batter, has a lofty dome to honor the *duomo* or cathedral in many a Lombardian town.

Food historian Waverley Root relates that it's a custom for the children of Milan to leave a bowl of panettone soaked in water on windowsills on New Year's Eve for the camels of the bearers of gifts to the Christ Child—much as American children leave Christmas Eve carrots for Santa's reindeer.

> 2 *packages active dry yeast*
> ½ *cup warm (105 to 115° F) water*
> ⅓ *cup sugar*
> ¼ *cup warm (105 to 115° F) milk*

> ½ *teaspoon salt*
> ¼ *teaspoon ground nutmeg*
> ⅔ *cup butter or margarine, softened*
> 2 *teaspoons grated orange rind*
> 1 *teaspoon vanilla extract*
> 3¾ *cups flour*
> 2 *eggs*
> 2 *egg yolks*
> ¼ *cup Marsala wine*
> ½ *cup golden raisins*
> ⅓ *cup each slivered candied cherries and diced mixed candied fruits*
> ¼ *cup pine nuts or slivered almonds*
> *Confectioners' sugar*

1. Sprinkle yeast over warm water in large bowl of an electric mixer; add 1 teaspoon of the sugar. Let stand until yeast is soft (about 5 minutes).

2. Add remaining sugar, warm milk, salt, nutmeg, butter, orange rind, and vanilla. Add 2 cups of the flour; mix to blend, then beat until smooth and elastic (about 5 minutes).

3. Beat in eggs and egg yolks, one at a time. Gradually beat in remaining 1¾ cups flour; when all has been added, beat at medium speed until batter is elastic (about 3 minutes).

4. Transfer batter to a greased bowl. Cover and let rise in a warm place until bubbly (about 1 hour). While batter is rising, pour Marsala over raisins in a small bowl; set aside.

5. Stir batter down; then stir in raisin mixture, cherries, candied fruits, and pine nuts until well distributed.

6. Spread batter in a well-greased, lightly floured, 9½- to 10-cup charlotte mold (about 7½ inches in diameter and 4 inches deep). Let rise until doubled (30 to 45 minutes). Preheat oven to 325° F.

7. Bake until bread is well browned and a skewer inserted in center comes out clean (1 to 1¼ hours). Let stand in pan on wire rack for about 15 minutes, then remove pan and transfer to rack to cool (rounded side up). Dust with confectioners' sugar while warm.

Makes 1 large coffee cake (10 to 12 servings).

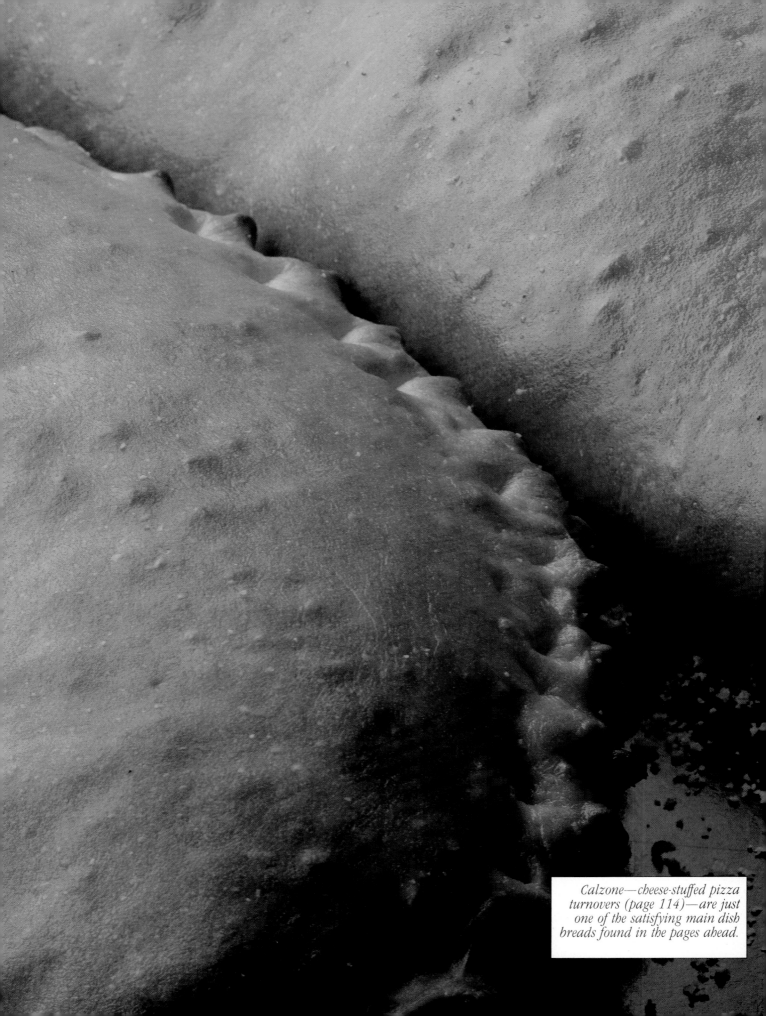

Calzone—cheese-stuffed pizza turnovers (page 114)—are just one of the satisfying main dish breads found in the pages ahead.

Main Dish Breads

Through the ages bread has been "the staff of life" in many cultures. Even today when most people consider bread to be only one part of a varied meal, bread-based main dishes command culinary attention. Say "Pizza for dinner!" and watch the smiles begin. Other crust-enclosed meals-in-one include hearty turnovers and filled breads such as calzone, pasties, and knishes. Northern Italian bakers take pride in rustic tortas stuffed with savory meats and cheeses. And diners are sure to be dazzled by bread-wrapped sausage, ham, or chicken.

PIZZA

Pizza is one of those foods almost everyone likes, whether or not he or she was lucky enough to have an Italian grandparent. Indeed, many of the pizzas of the eighties—lavished with such nontraditional toppings as caviar, duck breast, and smoked salmon—reveal few hints of their Neapolitan origin.

Making pizza at home offers some satisfying rewards. You can create just the kind of pizza you like best, varying the crust, too, with a measure of whole-grain flour. Or you can duplicate some of the popular restaurant forms—deep-dish pizza, double-crust "stuffed" pizza, and the fat pizza turnover called calzone.

Because waiting for pizza is no more fun at home than at a pizzeria, the dough chosen for all these pizzas is quick and easy to make. It uses fast-rising yeast and an efficient mixing method that doesn't require the yeast to be softened in liquid. If you wish, you can make the dough even faster in a food processor using a method that requires no hand kneading—the machine does it all.

Bread flour gives the crust, made by either method, a crisp elasticity. The Fresh Tomato Sauce for several of the pizzas can be made ahead—in quantity, during the summer when really ripe tomatoes are abundant—and frozen in anticipation of winter pizza baking.

PIZZA WITH RED ONION AND PANCETTA

This pizza and the four that follow it can be made in two sizes—in two 12-inch pans or one vast 17- to 18-inch pan. In either form, these pizzas will satisfy four famished pizza enthusiasts.

- *3 tablespoons olive oil*
- *1 large (about 10 oz) red onion, thinly slivered*
- *¼ pound pancetta (round Italian bacon), cut into ½-inch-wide strips*
- *3 cups (¾ lb) shredded whole-milk mozzarella cheese*
- *¼ cup grated pecorino, Romano, or Parmesan cheese*

Easy-Mix Pizza Dough

- *2⅓ to 2⅔ cups bread flour*
- *1 package fast-rising active dry yeast*
- *½ teaspoon salt*
- *1 cup hot (115° to 125° F) water*
- *1 teaspoon honey*
- *2 teaspoons olive oil*

Fresh Tomato Sauce

- *3 medium tomatoes (about 1 lb)*
- *2 tablespoons olive oil*
- *1 clove garlic, minced or pressed*
- *1 tablespoon chopped fresh basil or ½ teaspoon dried basil or herbes de Provence*
- *¼ teaspoon salt*
- *¼ cup dry white wine*

1. Prepare Easy-Mix Pizza Dough and let it rise.

2. While dough rises, make sauce, then set it aside.

3. Preheat oven to 450° F. Heat oil in a large frying pan over moderate heat. Add onion and cook, stirring often, until soft but not browned (8 to 10 minutes). Remove onion with a slotted spoon and reserve.

4. Add pancetta to same pan and cook, stirring often, until it begins to brown (about 3 minutes). Drain on paper towels, reserving oil in pan.

5. Grease two 11- to 12-inch pizza pans (or a single 17- to 18-inch pan). Divide dough into two equal portions; roll each half out to an 8-inch circle (or roll all of the dough to a 12- to 14-inch circle). Use your hands to pat and stretch dough to fit pans. Brush evenly with oil remaining in frying pan.

6. Divide sauce over the pizza(s). Sprinkle evenly with cheeses. Arrange onion and pancetta evenly over pizzas (or large, single pizza).

7. Bake on lowest rack of oven until crust browns well (15 to 20 minutes for small pizzas, 18 to 20 minutes for large, single pizza). Cut into wedges or squares and serve at once.

Makes 2 medium pizzas or 1 large pizza (4 to 6 servings).

Easy-Mix Pizza Dough

1. In large bowl of electric mixer combine 2 cups of the flour, yeast, and salt. Stir to blend dry ingredients thoroughly. In a small bowl combine hot water, honey, and oil; stir to blend well.

2. Add water mixture to flour mixture. Mix to blend, then beat at medium speed until smooth and elastic (about 5 minutes). Stir in about ⅓ cup more flour to make a soft dough. Turn dough out onto a generously floured board or pastry cloth. Knead until dough is smooth and satiny and small bubbles form just under surface (5 to 10 minutes), adding just enough bread flour (up to ⅓ cup) to prevent dough from being sticky.

3. Turn dough in a greased bowl. Cover with plastic wrap and a kitchen towel and let rise in a warm place until doubled in bulk (30 to 40 minutes). Punch dough down, cover with inverted bowl, and let rest 10 minutes, then use as directed.

Note Dough can also be prepared in food processor. In work bowl mix 2½ cups bread flour, yeast, and salt. Combine hot water, honey, and olive oil in a measuring cup. With machine running, pour water mixture through feed tube in a steady stream, adjusting amount poured so flour can absorb it. Turn off processor when dough forms a ball. Dough should feel a little sticky. If too soft, add more flour, 1 tablespoon at a time, until dough has a firm consistency. Knead by processing for an additional 45 seconds. Shape dough into a ball, then turn in a greased bowl to rise.

Fresh Tomato Sauce Pour boiling water over tomatoes; peel, then chop finely. Heat oil in a 2-quart saucepan over medium-high heat. Add tomatoes and garlic. Mix in basil, salt, and wine. Bring to a boil, cover, reduce heat, and simmer for 15 minutes. Uncover and cook over medium-high heat, stirring often as sauce begins to thicken, until sauce is thick and reduced to about 1 cup (15 to 20 minutes).

Pizza With Red Onion and Pancetta is flavored by the Italian-style bacon that's sliced like salami from a round loaf.

The fresh basil sauce called pesto is spooned over this savory pizza during its last moments in the oven, to keep the color a brilliant green.

PIZZA WITH PESTO, MUSHROOMS, AND FONTINA CHEESE

It's worth tucking away a jar or two of frozen pesto during the season of fresh basil so that later in the year you can make this irresistible meatless pizza.

Easy-Mix Pizza Dough (see page 108)

2 *tablespoons olive oil*

½ *pound mushrooms, thinly sliced*

3 *cups (¾ pound) shredded Fontina cheese*

Cinzia's Pesto

2 *cups lightly packed fresh basil leaves*

¼ *cup olive oil*

1 *teaspoon lemon juice*

1 *clove garlic, minced or pressed*

2 *tablespoons pine nuts (optional)*

⅔ *cup grated Parmesan cheese*

1. Prepare Easy-Mix Pizza Dough and let it rise.

2. While dough rises, make pesto, then set it aside to blend flavors.

3. Preheat oven to 450° F. Heat oil in a large frying pan over medium-high heat. Add mushrooms and cook, stirring often, until mushrooms are lightly browned and their liquid has cooked away. Remove pan from heat.

4. Divide dough into two equal portions; roll each half out to an 8-inch circle (or roll all of the dough to a 12- to 14-inch circle). Use your hands to pat and stretch dough to fit two greased 11- to 12-inch pizza pans (or a single 17- to 18-inch pizza pan). Brush evenly with some of the oil in which mushrooms were cooked.

5. Divide cheese over the two pizzas (or sprinkle it evenly over the large, single one). Arrange mushrooms evenly over cheese; drizzle with any remaining oil.

6. Bake on lowest rack of oven until crust browns well (15 to 20 minutes for small pizzas, about 25 minutes for large, single pizza). Spoon pesto evenly over pizza. Return to oven just long enough to heat pesto (1 to 2 minutes).

7. Cut into wedges or squares and serve at once.

Makes 2 medium pizzas or 1 large pizza (4 to 6 servings).

Cinzia's Pesto Rinse basil leaves well and pat dry before measuring. In blender or food processor combine oil, lemon juice, and garlic; add basil, pine nuts (if used), and cheese. Whirl or process until puréed.

Makes about ⅔ cup.

PIZZA NIÇOISE

Along the Côte d'Azur in southern France, pizza is as omnipresent as it is in Italy. Here is a version from Nice. It makes a pleasant informal meal with a green salad, light red wine, and fresh fruit for dessert.

> *Easy-Mix Pizza Dough (see page 108)*
> *Fresh Tomato Sauce (see page 108)*
> ¼ *cup olive oil*
> 2 *large onions, thinly slivered*
> 2 *cloves garlic, minced or pressed*
> ½ *teaspoon dried herbes de Provence*
> 2 *tablespoons chopped parsley*
> 2 *cups (½ lb) shredded whole-milk mozzarella cheese*
> 1 *can (2 oz) anchovy fillets, well drained*
> ¼ *cup small (unpitted) Niçoise olives*

1. Prepare Easy-Mix Pizza Dough and let it rise.

2. While dough rises, make Fresh Tomato Sauce, then set it aside.

3. Preheat oven to 450° F. Heat oil in a large frying pan over moderate heat. Add onions and cook, stirring often, until soft but not browned (10 to 12 minutes); remove from heat.

4. Spoon about 1 tablespoon of the hot oil from the pan into a small bowl; mix in garlic, herbes de Provence, and parsley.

5. Grease two 11- to 12-inch pizza pans (or a single 17- to 18-inch pizza pan) lightly. Divide dough into two equal portions; roll each half out to an 8-inch circle (or roll all of the dough to a 12- to 14-inch circle). Use your hands to pat and stretch dough to fit pans.

6. Divide sauce over the two pizzas (or spread it evenly over the large, single one). Sprinkle evenly with cheese. Spread onions over cheese. Arrange anchovies and olives over onions. Sprinkle evenly with garlic-and-herb mixture.

7. Bake on lowest rack of oven until crust browns well (15 to 20 minutes for small pizzas, 20 to 25 minutes for large, single pizza). Cut into wedges or squares and serve at once.

Makes 2 medium pizzas or 1 large pizza (4 to 6 servings).

GARLIC, GORGONZOLA, AND PROSCIUTTO PIZZA

The variety of savory Italian cheeses and delicatessen meats makes creating new pizza combinations a delicious mix-and-match game. This one teams blue-veined Gorgonzola and traditional whole-milk mozzarella cheese with prosciutto—the salty, air-dried ham native to Parma.

> *Easy-Mix Pizza Dough (see page 108)*
> *Fresh Tomato Sauce (see page 108)*
> 3 *cloves garlic (unpeeled)*
> 2 *cups boiling water*
> 2½ *cups (10 oz) shredded whole-milk mozzarella cheese*
> ½ *cup crumbled Gorgonzola cheese*
> ¼ *pound sliced prosciutto, cut into strips*

1. Prepare Easy-Mix Pizza Dough and let it rise.

2. While dough rises, make Fresh Tomato Sauce, then set it aside.

3. Preheat oven to 450° F. Add garlic to the boiling water in a small saucepan; boil for 1 minute. Drain, peel, then slice garlic thinly.

4. Grease two 11- to 12-inch pizza pans (or a single 17- to 18-inch pizza pan). Divide dough into two equal portions; roll each half out to an 8-inch circle (or roll all the dough to a 12- to 14-inch circle). Pat and stretch dough to fit pans.

5. Divide sauce over the two pizzas (or spread it evenly over the large, single one). Sprinkle with garlic, then with mozzarella, and finally Gorgonzola cheese, dividing all equally. Arrange half of the prosciutto strips over each pizza.

6. Bake on lowest rack of oven until crusts are well browned and cheese browns lightly (15 to 20 minutes for small pizzas, 18 to 20 minutes for large, single pizza). Cut into wedges or squares and serve at once.

Makes 2 medium pizzas or 1 large pizza (4 to 6 servings).

CHORIZO, CHEESE, AND GREEN CHILE PIZZA

For those who enjoy pizza even when it isn't more than vaguely Italian, here is a slightly *picante* version with a Mexican influence.

    3 tablespoons olive oil
    1 large onion, thinly slivered
    ½ teaspoon ground cumin
    ½ pound chorizo sausages
    3 cups (¾ lb) shredded
       Monterey jack cheese

Whole Wheat Pizza Dough

    2 to 2⅓ cups bread flour
    ⅓ cup whole wheat flour
    1 package fast-rising active
       dry yeast
    ½ teaspoon salt
    1 cup hot (115° to 125° F) water
    1 teaspoon honey
    2 teaspoons olive oil

Tomato and Green Chile Sauce

    3 medium tomatoes (about
       1 pound)
    2 tablespoons olive oil
    ¼ teaspoon dried oregano
    1 clove garlic, minced or pressed
    ¼ teaspoon salt
    1 can (4 oz) diced green chiles

1. Prepare Whole Wheat Pizza Dough and let it rise.

2. While dough rises, make Tomato and Green Chile Sauce, then set it aside.

3. Preheat oven to 450° F. Heat oil in a large frying pan over moderate heat. Add onion and cook, stirring often, until soft but not browned (8 to 10 minutes); mix in cumin, then transfer onion mixture (including oil) to a bowl.

4. Remove casings from sausages and crumble into same pan in which onions cooked. Cook, stirring often, until lightly browned. Remove sausage from pan with a slotted spoon and drain on paper towels.

5. Grease two 11- to 12-inch pizza pans (or one 17- to 18-inch pizza pan). Divide dough into two equal portions; roll each half out to an 8-inch circle (or roll all of the dough to a 12- to 14-inch circle). Use your hands to pat and stretch dough to fit pans.

6. Divide sauce over the two pizzas (or spread it evenly over the large, single one). Sprinkle evenly with cheese. Spread onions over cheese. Spoon sausage over onions.

7. Bake on lowest rack of oven until crust browns well (15 to 20 minutes for small pizzas, 20 to 25 minutes for large, single pizza). Cut into wedges or squares and serve at once.

Makes 2 medium pizzas or 1 large pizza (4 to 6 servings).

Whole Wheat Pizza Dough

1. In large bowl of electric mixer, combine 1⅔ cups of the bread flour, the whole wheat flour, yeast, and salt. Stir to blend dry ingredients thoroughly.

2. In a small bowl combine hot water, honey, and oil; stir to blend well. Add water mixture to flour mixture. Mix to blend, then beat at medium speed until smooth and elastic (about 5 minutes). Stir in about ⅓ cup more bread flour to make a soft dough.

3. Turn dough out onto a well-floured board or pastry cloth. Knead until dough is smooth under surface (5 to 10 minutes), adding just enough bread flour (up to ⅓ cup) to prevent dough from being sticky.

4. Turn dough in a greased bowl. Cover with plastic wrap and a towel and let rise in a warm place until doubled in bulk (30 to 40 minutes). Punch dough down, cover with inverted bowl, and let rest 10 minutes; then use as directed in recipe.

Tomato and Green Chile Sauce

Pour boiling water over tomatoes to loosen skins; peel, and chop finely.

Heat oil in a 2-quart saucepan over medium heat. Add tomatoes, oregano, garlic, salt, and green chiles. Bring to a boil, cover, reduce heat, and simmer for 15 minutes. Uncover and cook over medium-high heat, stirring often as sauce begins to thicken, until sauce is thick and reduced to about 1 cup (15 to 20 minutes).

DEEP-DISH PEPPERONI PIZZA

You'll need a special pan for this pizza and the double-crust variation that follows it. But once you've tried this huge, Chicago-style pizza, you'll realize the investment was wise. The pan resembles an oversize layer cake pan; it's 14 inches in diameter and about 2 inches deep. If you prefer, substitute browned, crumbled Italian sausage for the pepperoni.

    4   cups (1 lb) shredded
        mozzarella cheese
    1   can (2¼ oz) sliced ripe
        olives, well drained
    2½ cups (about ½ lb)
        thinly sliced pepperoni
    ⅔   cup grated Parmesan cheese

Deep-Dish Pizza Dough

    3   to 3½ cups unbleached
        all-purpose flour
    1   package fast-rising active
        dry yeast
    ¾   teaspoon salt
    1¼ cups hot (115° to 125° F)
        water
    2   teaspoons honey
    1   tablespoon olive oil

Tomato-Mushroom Sauce

    2   tablespoons olive oil
    1   large onion, finely chopped
    ¼   pound mushrooms,
        thinly sliced
    1   clove garlic minced or pressed
    1   can (14½ oz) Italian-style
        tomatoes, coarsely chopped
    ¼   cup tomato paste
    ¼   teaspoon each salt,
        pepper, and dried oregano
    1   teaspoon dried basil

1. Prepare Deep-Dish Pizza Dough and let it rise.

2. While dough rises, make Tomato-Mushroom Sauce, then set it aside.

3. Preheat oven to 450° F. Grease a 14-inch deep-dish pizza pan (about 2 inches deep). Roll dough out on a floured surface to about a 14-inch circle. Use your hands to pat and stretch dough to fit into pan, pressing it against sides of pan to reach top edge.

4. Sprinkle half the mozzarella cheese over bottom of dough. Add olives in an even layer, then pepperoni. Spread evenly with sauce. Cover with remaining mozzarella cheese, then sprinkle with Parmesan cheese.

5. Bake on lowest rack of oven until crust browns well and cheese is richly browned (25 to 30 minutes). Cut into wedges and serve at once.

Makes 1 large pizza, about 6 servings.

Deep-Dish Pizza Dough

1. In large bowl of electric mixer, combine 2½ cups of the flour, yeast, and salt. Stir to blend dry ingredients thoroughly. In a small bowl combine the hot water, honey, and oil; stir to blend well.

2. Add water mixture to flour mixture. Mix to blend, then beat at medium speed until smooth and elastic (about 5 minutes). Stir in about ½ cup more flour to make a soft dough.

3. Turn dough out onto a floured board or pastry cloth. Knead until dough is smooth and satiny and small bubbles form just under surface (8 to 10 minutes), adding just enough flour (up to ½ cup) to prevent dough from being sticky.

4. Turn dough in a greased bowl. Cover with plastic wrap and a towel and let rise in a warm place until doubled in bulk (30 to 40 minutes). Punch dough down, cover with inverted bowl, and let rest for 10 minutes; use as directed in recipe.

Tomato-Mushroom Sauce In a 2- to 3-quart saucepan heat oil over medium heat; add onion and mushrooms. Cook, stirring often, until onion is soft and mushrooms brown lightly. Mix in garlic, tomatoes with their juice, tomato paste, salt, pepper, oregano, and basil. Bring to a boil, cover, reduce heat, and simmer for 20 minutes. Uncover, increase heat so sauce boils gently, and continue cooking until sauce is thickened and reduced to about 2½ cups (12 to 15 minutes).

Serve a green vegetable such as broccoli to complement a dinner of hot Pork-and-Veal-Stuffed Yeast Pasties (page 115).

STUFFED VEGETARIAN PIZZA

Students of pizza trace the "stuffed" pizza concept to Giordano's on Chicago's South Side. But like *nouvelle cuisine*, the idea has been carried far and wide by alumni of that restaurant's kitchen. It involves lining a deep-dish pizza pan with about half of the dough, adding layers of cheese and filling, and topping it with the rest of the crust. Then come crowning layers of tomato sauce and more cheese.

This vegetable-filled adaptation is abundantly hearty, but you could flavor it with strips of salami, sliced pepperoni, or crumbles of sautéed Italian sausage if you prefer.

> *Deep-Dish Pizza Dough (see page 112)*
> *Fresh Tomato Sauce (see page 108)*
> ¼ *cup olive oil*
> 1 *large onion, thinly slivered*
> ½ *pound mushrooms, thinly sliced*
> 1 *red or green bell pepper, quartered, seeded, and cut in thin strips*
> 2 *cloves garlic, minced or pressed*
> ½ *teaspoon each salt and dried oregano*
> ⅛ *teaspoon each pepper and dried marjoram*
> 4 *cups (1 lb) shredded Monterey jack cheese*
> ⅔ *cup grated Parmesan or Romano cheese*

1. Prepare Deep-Dish Pizza Dough and let it rise.

2. While dough rises, make Fresh Tomato Sauce, then set it aside.

3. Preheat oven to 450° F. While dough rises, heat oil in a large frying pan over medium-high heat. Add onion, mushrooms, and red pepper.

Cook, stirring often, until onion is soft, mushrooms brown lightly, and any mushroom liquid evaporates. Mix in garlic, salt, oregano, pepper, and marjoram, then remove from heat.

4. Grease a 14-inch deep-dish pizza pan (about 2 inches deep). Divide dough into two portions, one about a third larger than the other. Roll larger portion of dough out on a floured surface to about a 14-inch circle. Use your hands to pat and stretch dough to fit into pan, pressing it against sides of pan to reach top edge.

5. Sprinkle evenly with 3 cups of the jack cheese. Spread vegetable mixture over cheese.

6. Roll out remaining dough to a 14-inch circle; place over vegetables, pressing edge against dough already in pan. Fold dough lining pan over top layer.

7. Spread tomato sauce over top layer of dough. Sprinkle evenly with remaining 1 cup jack cheese. Top with Parmesan cheese.

8. Bake on lowest rack of oven until crust browns well and cheese is richly browned (25 to 30 minutes). Let stand for 2 to 3 minutes before cutting into wedges to serve.

Makes 1 large pizza, 4 to 6 servings.

CALZONE AND OTHER TURNOVERS

Nearly every culture offers an example of meat and other savory fillings enclosed in dough. Some of the most enjoyable are wrapped in yeast pastries. Unlike a flaky, short-crust pastry, yeast dough is elastic enough to stretch to virtually any shape without tearing, and it puffs invitingly during baking.

CALZONE WITH SUN-DRIED TOMATOES

Years before pizza became a trendy example of "California cuisine," a San Francisco pizzeria called Lupo's astonished its habitués with *calzone imbottito*. According to food historian Waverley Root, this form of pizza turnover originated in Naples—but it never tasted more wonderful than when it came from Lupo's brick ovens. Calzone is named for the trouser leg some people think it resembles.

> *Deep-Dish Pizza Dough (see page 112)*
> 1 *tablespoon oil from sun-dried tomatoes*
> 1 *medium onion, finely chopped*
> 1 *clove garlic, minced or pressed*
> 1 *cup (8 oz) ricotta cheese*
> ¼ *cup chopped sun-dried tomatoes*
> 2 *tablespoons chopped fresh parsley*
> ¼ *pound sliced prosciutto or dry salami, cut into strips*
> 2 *cups (½ lb) shredded whole-milk mozzarella cheese*
> *Cornmeal (for baking sheet)*
> *Olive oil*

1. Prepare Deep-Dish Pizza Dough and let it rise.

2. While dough rises, prepare filling. In a medium frying pan heat tomato oil over moderate heat; add onion and cook, stirring often, until soft but not browned. Mix in garlic, then remove from heat.

3. In a medium bowl mix ricotta cheese with dried tomatoes and parsley; stir in cooked onion mixture.

4. Divide dough into two equal portions. Roll each half out on a floured surface to a 12-inch circle. Spread half of the ricotta filling over half of each circle of dough, leaving about a ½-inch margin.

5. Sprinkle half of each circle with half of the prosciutto strips and 1 cup of the mozzarella cheese. Fold circles in halves over filling, moistening and pinching edges together (or pressing with tines of a fork) to seal.

6. Preheat oven to 450° F. Sprinkle a large, greased baking sheet lightly with cornmeal. Place calzone well apart on prepared baking sheet. Let rise until puffy (12 to 15 minutes).

7. Bake on center rack until crust browns well (about 15 minutes). Brush tops lightly with olive oil, then serve hot.

Makes 2 calzone, 4 servings.

PORK-AND-VEAL-STUFFED YEAST PASTIES

Legend has it that the pasty (pronounced PAS tee) was created for Cornish miners to carry in their lunch boxes. Pasty vendors in St. Ives will tell you that sometimes they're made with a savory filling at one end and a sweet apple one at the other—entrée and dessert baked in a single crust! This version opts for strictly meat and potatoes, but you might use the same oven to bake apples to follow the turnovers as dessert.

1 large (about ¾ lb) boiling potato, well scrubbed and cut lengthwise into quarters
1 pound ground pork, crumbled
½ pound ground veal, crumbled
1 large carrot, finely chopped
2 medium onions, finely chopped
1 clove garlic, minced or pressed
1 teaspoon salt
½ teaspoon dried sage
¼ teaspoon each pepper, ground allspice, and dried thyme
¼ cup chopped parsley
1 egg, beaten with 1 tablespoon milk

Pasty Yeast Pastry

3¼ to 4 cups unbleached all-purpose flour
1 package fast-rising active dry yeast
½ teaspoon salt
1½ cups hot (115° to 125° F) water
2 teaspoons honey
1 tablespoon butter or margarine, softened

1. Cover potato with water in a small saucepan, bring to a boil, cover, and boil gently until just tender (12 to 15 minutes). Drain; cut potato into ½-inch cubes.

2. While potato cooks, prepare Pasty Yeast Pastry and let it rise.

3. Place pork and veal in a large frying pan. Cook over medium heat, stirring often, until meat releases a film of fat, then add carrot, onions, garlic, salt, sage, pepper, allspice, and thyme. Cook, stirring often, until meats and onions brown lightly. Remove from heat and stir in potato and parsley. (If done ahead, cover and refrigerate.)

4. Divide dough into 8 equal portions. Roll each out on a floured surface to an 8-inch circle. In center of each place an eighth (about ¾ cup) of the filling.

5. Lift up two parallel sides of each circle and bring together in middle (over center of filling). Moisten edges, then pinch or crimp to seal in a line down center of pasty.

6. Preheat oven to 450° F. Place pasties well apart on a large, greased, rimmed baking sheet. Brush lightly with egg mixture. Let rise until dough looks puffy (12 to 15 minutes).

7. Bake until pasties are well browned (12 to 15 minutes). Serve hot or warm.

Makes 8 pasties.

Pasty Yeast Pastry

1. In large electric mixer bowl combine 2¾ cups of the flour, yeast, and salt. Stir to blend dry ingredients thoroughly. In a small bowl combine the hot water, honey, and butter; stir to blend well.

2. Add water mixture to flour mixture. Mix to blend, then beat at medium speed until smooth and elastic (about 5 minutes). Stir in about ½ cup more unbleached flour to make a soft dough.

3. Turn dough out onto a floured board or pastry cloth. Knead until dough is smooth and satiny and small bubbles form just under surface (10 to 12 minutes), adding just enough unbleached flour (up to ¾ cup) to prevent dough from being sticky.

4. Turn dough in a greased bowl. Cover with plastic wrap and a kitchen towel and let rise in a warm place until doubled in bulk (30 to 40 minutes). Punch dough down, cover with an inverted bowl, and let rest for 10 minutes; then use as directed in recipe.

TRADITIONAL BEEF-AND-POTATO KNISHES

The meat-filled pastry of Jewish cooking tradition is the *knish*. The fat used in the dough and for sautéing the onions in the filling is melted chicken fat, or *Schmalz*. While salad oil can also be used, it doesn't impart the rich flavor and golden color of chicken fat. Schmalz is available from a poultry dealer or prepare it yourself from the tufts of fat pulled from the cavity of a whole chicken. Chop the fat coarsely, place in a 1- to 1½-quart saucepan over low heat, and cook until most of the fat is melted and only a few crisp solids remain. Strain them out, and the fat is ready. You'll get about 1 cup from ½ pound of chicken fat.

> 1 boneless beef chuck roast or brisket (2 to 2½ lbs)
> 1 bay leaf
> ⅛ teaspoon whole black peppercorns
> 2 medium-sized boiling potatoes (about 1 lb total), peeled and cut in quarters
> About ½ cup melted chicken fat or salad oil
> 2 medium onions, finely chopped
> 2 teaspoons salt
> ⅛ teaspoon white pepper
> 1 egg, slightly beaten

Knish Dough

> 3¼ to 3¾ cups unbleached all-purpose flour
> 1 package fast-acting active dry yeast
> ½ teaspoon salt
> 1 tablespoon sugar
> ¾ cup hot (115° to 125° F) water
> ¼ cup melted chicken fat or salad oil
> 2 eggs

1. Preheat oven to 500° F. Place beef, fat side up, in a shallow roasting pan. Bake, uncovered, until well browned (15 to 20 minutes). Transfer beef to a 4- to 5-quart kettle. Add a little water to roasting pan, stirring to loosen drippings; pour over beef.

2. To beef add bay leaf and black peppercorns, then more water to cover. Bring to a boil over medium heat, cover, reduce heat, and simmer until beef is tender (2½ to 3 hours).

3. When beef is tender, cook potatoes in boiling water to cover until tender (12 to 15 minutes); drain well. Using a potato masher or electric mixer, beat potatoes until fluffy, adding up to 1 tablespoon of the chicken fat if very dry.

4. Cook onions in 2 tablespoons of the chicken fat in a medium frying pan over moderate heat until soft but not browned; remove from heat and add to potatoes.

5. Remove beef from liquid (reserve and freeze liquid, if you wish, to use as broth when making soup). Cool beef slightly. Cut into chunks and grind, using medium blade of food chopper or food processor. (You should have about 4 cups ground cooked beef.)

6. Complete filling by combining ground cooked beef in a large bowl with potato mixture, salt, pepper, and egg; mix to combine thoroughly.

7. Divide dough into three equal portions. Cover two of them with plastic wrap to prevent dough from becoming dry. Roll one third of the dough out on a lightly floured surface to a 10- by 16-inch rectangle. Brush dough with some of the remaining chicken fat. Shape a third of the beef filling into a long roll about 1 inch from a 16-inch edge. Roll dough securely around filling. Pinch long edge to seal.

8. Repeat filling process two more times, using another third of the filling for each. As each roll is completed, cover with plastic wrap to keep it moist.

9. Cut each filled roll of dough into 1-inch slices. Stretch dough up and over cut edges and seal in center, enclosing filling on all sides.

10. Preheat oven to 375° F. Place knishes well apart on greased baking sheets. Brush lightly with chicken fat. Let rise until dough looks puffy (20 to 30 minutes).

11. Bake until knishes are golden brown (15 to 20 minutes).

Makes 4 dozen knishes.

Knish Dough

1. In large bowl of electric mixer, combine 2 cups of the flour, yeast, salt, and sugar. Stir to blend dry ingredients thoroughly. In a small bowl combine water and chicken fat; stir to blend well. Add water mixture to flour mixture. Mix to blend, then beat at medium speed until smooth and elastic (about 5 minutes). Add eggs, one at a time, beating well after each addition. Stir in about 1¼ cups more flour to make a soft dough.

2. Turn dough out onto a floured board or pastry cloth. Knead until smooth and satiny and small bubbles form just under surface (8 to 10 minutes), adding just enough unbleached flour (up to ½ cup) to prevent dough from being sticky.

3. Turn dough in a greased bowl. Cover with plastic wrap and a kitchen towel and let rise in a warm place until doubled in bulk (30 to 40 minutes). Punch dough down, cover with inverted bowl, and let rest for 10 minutes; use as directed in recipe.

Note Filling can be prepared up to a day in advance, covered, and refrigerated. Dough can be prepared through the first rising, covered, and refrigerated to rise. Fill, shape, and bake knishes the second day.

To freeze baked knishes, cool on wire racks, then wrap in heavy foil. Take foil-wrapped packages from freezer and reheat in a 350° F oven for about 45 minutes.

Beef-and-Potato Knishes make a great lunch with soup. If baked ahead and frozen, they can be reheated and served appetizingly warm.

RUSTIC FRENCH SUPPER

Green Salad

Ham, Pâté, and Mushroom Turnovers

Winter Vegetable Soup

Gratin of Three Fruits

Red Wine

Coffee

These ample, wheat-crusted turnovers are a synthesis of two traditions—the prosciutto-filled piadine *of Turin in Italy's northwest and the pastry-wrapped truffles (*truffes sous les cendres) *of France's southwest. They can be made ahead and refrigerated or frozen, then warmed in the oven to accompany the creamy green soup.*

HAM, PÂTÉ, AND MUSHROOM TURNOVERS

> 3 tablespoons butter or margarine
> 1 tablespoon salad oil
> 1 pound mushrooms, thinly sliced
> 1 shallot, finely chopped
>   Pinch each *white pepper* and *dried tarragon*
> 2 teaspoons lemon juice
> 6 thin slices prosciutto
> ¼ pound chicken liver pâté at room temperature
> 1 egg yolk, beaten with 1 tablespoon water

Whole Wheat Turnover Dough

> 2¾ to 3¼ cups bread flour
> ½ cup whole wheat flour
> 1 package fast-rising active dry yeast
> ½ teaspoon salt
> 1½ cups hot (115° to 125° F) water
> 2 teaspoons honey
> 1 tablespoon salad oil

1. Prepare Whole Wheat Turnover Dough and let it rise. While dough rises, melt butter with oil in a large frying pan over medium-high heat. Add mushrooms and shallot; cook, stirring often, until mushrooms brown lightly. Add pepper, tarragon, and lemon juice; stir until any liquid has evaporated; then remove from heat.

2. Divide dough into six equal portions. Roll each out on a floured surface to an 8-inch circle. On each place a slice of prosciutto, folding to fit over half of the round.

3. Beat pâté in a small bowl until it is soft enough to spread easily. Spread a generous tablespoon of the pâté over each slice of prosciutto.

4. Spoon a sixth of the mushroom mixture over each portion of pâté.

5. Fold circles in halves over filling, moistening and pinching edges together (or pressing with tines of a fork) to seal.

6. Preheat oven to 450° F. Place turnovers well apart on a large, greased baking sheet. Brush lightly with egg yolk mixture. Let rise until dough looks puffy (12 to 15 minutes).

7. Bake until turnovers are well browned (12 to 15 minutes). Serve hot.

Makes 6 turnovers.

Whole Wheat Turnover Dough

1. In large bowl of electric mixer, combine 2¼ cups of the bread flour, the whole wheat flour, yeast, and salt. Stir to blend dry ingredients thoroughly.

2. In a small bowl combine the hot water, honey, and oil; blend well.

3. Add water mixture to flour mixture. Mix to blend, then beat at medium speed until smooth and elastic (about 5 minutes). Stir in about ½ cup more bread flour to make a soft dough.

4. Turn dough out onto a floured board or pastry cloth. Knead until dough is smooth and satiny and small bubbles form just under surface (5 to 10 minutes), adding just enough bread flour (up to ½ cup) to prevent dough from being sticky.

5. Turn dough in a greased bowl. Cover with plastic wrap and a kitchen towel and let rise in a warm place until doubled in bulk (30 to 40 minutes). Punch dough down, cover with inverted bowl, and let rest for 10 minutes; use as directed in recipe.

WINTER VEGETABLE SOUP

  3 tablespoons butter or
     margarine
  ½ cup chopped shallots
  1 stalk celery, thinly sliced
  1 small carrot, thinly sliced
  1 small boiling potato, diced
  3 medium turnips (about 1 lb),
     peeled and coarsely chopped
  2 cups lightly packed, coarsely
     chopped Swiss chard leaves
     (discard coarse stems)
  ⅛ teaspoon white pepper
  ¼ teaspoon dried marjoram
     Pinch cayenne pepper
3½ cups chicken or beef broth
     (2 cans, 14½ oz each)
  1 cup half-and-half
     Salt (optional)

1. Melt butter in a 3-quart saucepan over medium heat. Add shallots, celery, and carrot; cook, stirring occasionally, until soft but not browned. Mix in potato, turnips, chard, pepper, marjoram, cayenne, and broth.

2. Bring to a boil, reduce heat, cover, and simmer until turnips are very tender (12 to 15 minutes).

3. Whirl mixture in blender or food processor, about half at a time, until smooth.

4. Return to cooking pan, add half-and-half, and reheat to serving temperature. (Do not boil.) Taste and add salt, if needed. Serve hot.

Makes 7 to 8 cups, about 6 servings.

GRATIN OF THREE FRUITS

  1 cup dry white wine
  ½ cup sugar
  4 firm medium to large
     pears, peeled, quartered
     lengthwise, and cored
  ¼ teaspoon vanilla extract
  2 navel oranges, peeled
     and segmented
  2 cups seedless red grapes
     (or halved, seeded grapes)

Custard Sauce

  1 tablespoon cornstarch
  ½ cup sugar
     Pinch each salt and
     ground nutmeg
  ¼ cup whipping cream
  ¾ cup half-and-half
  4 egg yolks
  ¼ teaspoon grated lemon rind
  1 tablespoon pear brandy
     or rum

1. In a 2-quart saucepan combine wine and sugar. Bring mixture to a boil over high heat, stirring until sugar dissolves.

2. Add pears to wine mixture. Cover, reduce heat, and simmer, turning pears occasionally to cover with liquid, until they are just tender when pierced with a fork (6 to 8 minutes).

3. In blender or food processor combine 6 of the pear quarters, 2 tablespoons of the poaching liquid, and vanilla. Whirl or process until puréed. Pour into a shallow, oval 6-cup gratin pan or baking dish.

4. Slice remaining cooked pears and arrange in purée in baking dish. Add orange segments and grapes. (If done ahead, cover and refrigerate for up to 6 hours; remove from refrigerator about 30 minutes before serving.)

5. Shortly before serving, prepare Custard Sauce, preheat broiler; pour sauce evenly over fruits. Broil about 4 inches from heat until top begins to brown lightly (3 to 4 minutes). Serve at once.

Serves 6.

Custard Sauce In a heavy saucepan mix cornstarch, sugar, salt, and nutmeg. Blend in whipping cream, then half-and-half; cook over medium heat, stirring constantly, until thick. In a small bowl, beat egg yolks with grated lemon rind. Beat in a little of the hot sauce, then return to remaining cream sauce over low heat and stir just until thick (3 to 5 minutes; do not boil). Remove from heat and blend in brandy or rum.

This Italian country torta is filled with Italian sausage, sliced tomato, and Fontina cheese. Serve warm with marinated yellow peppers in a green salad.

ITALIAN COUNTRY TORTAS

The countryside of Lombardy—and, indeed, much of rural Italy—produces fanciful combinations of bread and fillings in a variety of forms. Made with lighter, thicker dough than pizza, they are known (in the singular form) as *torta rustica.*

Typically, each torta has a savory filling sandwiched between two layers of yeast dough. Served hot, warm, or at room temperature, such a torta makes a pleasant brunch, lunch, or supper when accompanied by assorted antipasti, a light soup, a leafy salad, or fruit. Choose appropriate side dishes to suit the season and the time of day.

EGGPLANT, PEPPER, AND ARTICHOKE TORTA

A deep-dish torta with a whole wheat crust encloses the vegetable filling.

- ¼ cup olive oil
- 1 small eggplant (about 1 lb), cut in ½-inch (unpeeled) cubes
- 1 small onion, finely chopped
- 1 sweet red or green bell pepper, quartered, seeded, and cut into thin strips
- 2 cloves garlic, minced or pressed
- 1 teaspoon dried basil
- ½ teaspoon each *salt and dried oregano*
- ¼ teaspoon pepper
- 1 package (9 oz) frozen artichoke hearts
- 1 can (14½ oz) Italian-style tomatoes, coarsely chopped
- 3 eggs
- 1 cup (¼ pound) shredded Swiss cheese
- 2 tablespoons grated Parmesan cheese

Wheat Dough

- 1 package active dry yeast
- ¼ cup warm (105° to 115° F) water
- 1 tablespoon honey
- ½ teaspoon salt
- 1½ cups unbleached all-purpose flour
- 2 eggs
- ½ cup whole wheat flour
- ½ cup butter or margarine, softened

1. Prepare Wheat Dough, and while it is rising, make filling.

2. Heat oil over medium heat in a large (at least 12 inches) frying pan. Add eggplant, onion, and red pepper. Cook, stirring often, until onion is soft and begins to brown.

3. Mix in garlic, basil, salt, oregano, pepper, and artichokes. Add tomatoes and their liquid.

4. Bring mixture to a boil, then reduce heat so mixture boils gently. Cook, stirring occasionally, until eggplant is tender and liquid has evaporated (15 to 20 minutes). Remove from heat and let cool slightly.

5. Beat two of the eggs in a large bowl. Add vegetable mixture and Swiss cheese; mix lightly to blend.

6. Shape about two thirds of the dough into a ball on a well-floured surface. Roll out to about a 14-inch circle. Line a well-greased 8-inch springform pan with dough.

7. Spread vegetable mixture in dough-lined pan. Fold in dough at edge, over filling. Roll remaining third of the dough out to make a 9-inch square; cut into 1-inch-wide strips. Weave strips over filling to make a lattice pattern, tucking ends of dough down around dough lining edge of pan.

8. Preheat oven to 375° F. Let torta rise until it looks puffy (15 to 20 minutes). Beat remaining egg with 1 teaspoon water; brush over lattice topping. Sprinkle evenly with Parmesan cheese.

9. Bake until dough is richly browned and filling is set (50 minutes to 1 hour). Cool in pan on a wire rack for about 10 minutes before removing sides of pan. Cut into wedges and serve warm or at room temperature.

Serves 6 to 8.

Wheat Dough

1. Sprinkle yeast over warm water in large bowl of electric mixer; add honey. Let stand until yeast is soft (about 5 minutes). Mix in salt and ½ cup of the unbleached flour. Beat at medium speed until elastic (about 3 minutes).

2. Beat in eggs, one at a time, until smooth. Gradually beat in whole wheat flour and remaining 1 cup unbleached flour to make a soft dough. Beat in butter, a tablespoon at a time, beating well after each addition.

3. Place dough in a greased bowl, cover, and let rise in a warm place until doubled in bulk (1 to 1½ hours). Stir dough down, cover, and let rest for 10 minutes.

SPINACH AND CHEESE TORTA RUSTICA

A latticework of puffy strips tops this colorful vegetarian torta. The dough is rich, buttery, and almost like a brioche. As a variation, layer cooked Italian sausage, sliced tomato, and Fontina cheese to fill the torta. Shape the top layer of dough into triangular wedges to give a different look.

> 1 package (10 oz) frozen chopped spinach
> 2 tablespoons olive oil
> 1 small onion, finely chopped
> 1 clove garlic, minced or pressed
> 1 egg yolk
> 1 cup whole-milk ricotta cheese
> ½ cup grated Parmesan cheese
> ½ teaspoon salt
> ⅛ teaspoon pepper
> Pinch ground nutmeg
> 1 egg, beaten with 1 teaspoon water
> 2 tablespoons grated Parmesan cheese

Torta Dough

> 1 package active dry yeast
> ¼ cup warm (105° to 115° F) water
> 1 tablespoon honey
> ½ teaspoon salt
> 2 cups unbleached all-purpose flour
> 2 eggs
> ½ cup butter or margarine, softened

1. Prepare Torta Dough and while it is rising, make filling.

2. Thaw spinach. Drain, pressing out as much moisture as possible. In a small frying pan over medium heat, heat oil. Add onion and cook, stirring often, until lightly browned; mix in garlic; remove from heat.

3. In a medium bowl beat the egg yolk. Blend in ricotta cheese, then add the ½ cup Parmesan cheese, salt, pepper, nutmeg, and spinach and onion mixture. Mix to blend.

4. Divide Torta Dough into two portions, one slightly larger than the other. Roll out larger portion on a floured surface to make an 8-inch circle.

5. Fit circle of dough into a well-greased 8-inch springform pan. Spread evenly with filling. Roll remaining dough out to make a 9-inch square; cut into 1-inch-wide strips. Weave strips over filling to make a lattice pattern, tucking ends of dough down around filling.

6. Preheat oven to 375° F. Let torta rise until it looks puffy (15 to 20 minutes). Brush with the beaten egg mixture; sprinkle evenly with the 2 tablespoons Parmesan cheese.

7. Bake until dough is richly browned (40 to 45 minutes). Cool torta in pan for about 5 minutes, then remove rim. Serve warm or at room temperature, cut into wedges.

Serves 6 to 8.

Torta Dough

1. Sprinkle yeast over warm water in large bowl of an electric mixer; add honey. Let stand until yeast is soft (about 5 minutes). Mix in salt and ½ cup of the flour. Beat at medium speed until elastic (about 3 minutes).

2. Beat in the 2 eggs, one at a time, until smooth. Gradually beat in the remaining 1½ cups flour to make a soft dough. Beat in butter, 1 tablespoon at a time, beating well after each addition.

3. Transfer dough to a greased bowl, cover, and let rise in a warm place until doubled in bulk (about 1 hour). Stir dough down.

A warm brioche loaf surrounds slices of garlicky Italian-style coteghino *sausage. It makes a good first course or buffet dish.*

GARLIC SAUSAGE IN BRIOCHE LOAF

French restaurants serve sausage centered in a slice of brioche as a first course, but the dish need not be so restricted. It is also a handsome centerpiece for a small buffet of hot and cold foods. The bread has a tendency to separate from the sausage as it bakes, but Paula Wolfert (attributing the *truc* to the Paris pastry school, Lenôtre) suggests painting both bread and sausage with beaten egg yolk, then sprinkling lightly with flour. The sausage called *coteghino* (or *cotechino*), found in Italian delicatessens, is a close cousin to the fat garlic sausages used to make this dish in France.

> 1 coteghino sausage (1 to 1½ lbs)
> 1 bay leaf
> ¼ teaspoon whole black peppercorns
>   Torta Dough (see page 121)
> 2 egg yolks, beaten with 2 teaspoons water
>   Additional flour

1. Pierce sausage in several places with a fork. Place in a deep 3½- to 4-quart kettle or Dutch oven with bay leaf and peppercorns. Cover with water. Bring to a boil over medium heat. Cover, reduce heat, and simmer for 45 minutes. Remove sausage from cooking liquid. When cool enough to handle, carefully remove casing.

2. While sausage cooks, prepare Torta Dough and let it rise.

3. Roll dough out on a generously floured surface to make a rectangle about 9 by 16 inches. Brush lightly with some of the egg yolk mixture. Dust lightly with additional flour. Brush egg yolk mixture over cooked sausage and dust it with flour. Cover and reserve remaining egg yolk mixture.

BREAD-WRAPPED MEATS

A large, whole cut of meat or poultry baked in a pastry or bread enclosure evokes visions of sumptuous banquets of old—of "four and twenty blackbirds baked in a pie."
Such impressive presentations continue even today in restaurants featuring wheeled serving carts laden with whole fillets of beef Wellington.

While many such dishes are indeed feats of such magnitude that only a large restaurant or well-equipped caterer should attempt them, others can be handled without undue difficulty at home. Here are three.

4. Place sausage at one end of a narrow side of dough, about 1 inch in from end. Roll jelly-roll fashion, to other end of dough. Pinch dough to seal ends. Place, with long sealed edge at bottom, in a well-greased 4½- by 8½-inch loaf pan.

5. Cover lightly and let rise in a warm place until dough looks puffy (about 30 minutes). (Or, if made ahead, cover and refrigerate for several hours or overnight; remove from refrigerator and let rise until dough looks puffy, about 1 hour, before baking.)

6. Preheat oven to 350° F. Brush dough lightly with remaining egg yolk mixture. Bake until well browned (45 minutes to 1 hour).

7. Place pan (with loaf) on a wire rack and let stand for about 15 minutes; then carefully remove loaf from pan and cut into ½-inch slices. Serve warm.

Serves 4 to 6.

HAM IN EGG BREAD

In the Alsace region of eastern France, a whole ham is sometimes baked in a shell of bread dough and served at a large gathering. Some bakers prepare it so realistically that the small end is decorated to look like a pig's face. Without taking quite such elaborate measures, you can still produce a stunning creation using a 5-pound boneless ham.

> 1 round or oval fully-cooked boneless ham (4½ to 5 lbs)
> 1 cup water
> ½ cup firmly packed brown sugar
> 2 tablespoons Dijon mustard
> 2 teaspoons tarragon white wine vinegar
> 1 teaspoon Worcestershire sauce
> ⅛ teaspoon each *ground allspice and ground ginger*
> Flour
> 1 egg, beaten with 1 tablespoon water

Egg Bread Dough

> 1 package active dry yeast
> ¼ cup warm (105° to 115° F) water
> 1 teaspoon sugar
> ½ cup warm water
> ½ teaspoon salt
> 1 tablespoon salad oil
> 2¾ to 3 cups flour
> 1 egg

Nippy Whipped Cream

> 1 cup whipping cream
> 1 tablespoon lemon juice
> 1½ teaspoons Dijon mustard
> ⅛ teaspoon salt
> Pinch white pepper
> 2 tablespoons prepared horseradish

1. Preheat oven to 325° F. Place ham on a rack in a shallow baking pan. Pour water into bottom of pan. Bake, uncovered, for 45 minutes. Turn ham and bake for 30 minutes more.

2. While ham bakes, in a small bowl mix brown sugar, mustard, vinegar, Worcestershire sauce, allspice, and ginger until smoothly combined.

3. Prepare Egg Bread Dough and let it rise.

4. Brush ham generously with brown sugar mixture and continue baking until well browned (30 to 45 minutes). Reserve remaining brown sugar mixture. Refrigerate baked ham until it is cool to the touch (about 30 minutes).

5. Remove and discard any netting from ham. Brush again with some of the reserved brown sugar mixture. Sprinkle lightly with flour.

6. Roll dough out on a floured surface to a 12- by 18-inch rectangle. Trim evenly, reserving scraps for decoration, if you wish. Spread dough with remaining brown sugar mixture, leaving a 1-inch margin on all sides. Place ham in center of rectangle, top side down. Wrap dough securely around ham, pressing it against surface. Moisten edges of dough and pinch together firmly to seal across center and ends.

7. Place dough-wrapped ham, seam side down, on a greased rimmed baking sheet. Decorate dough, if desired, with design cut from trimmings. (If made ahead, cover lightly and refrigerate for up to 24 hours, until about 1 hour before baking.)

8. Let stand until dough looks puffy (30 minutes to 1 hour). Brush lightly with egg mixture.

9. Preheat oven to 350° F and bake until bread is well browned (45 to 50 minutes). Let stand for 10 to 15 minutes, then cut into about ½-inch slices. Serve hot with Nippy Whipped Cream.

Serves 8 to 10.

Egg Bread Dough

1. Sprinkle yeast over the ¼ cup warm water in large bowl of electric mixer. Add sugar. Let stand until yeast is soft (about 5 minutes). Stir in the ½ cup warm water, salt, and oil.

2. Add 1½ cups of the flour. Mix to blend, then beat at medium speed until smooth and elastic (about 5 minutes). Add egg and beat until smooth. Gradually stir in about 1 cup more flour to make a soft dough. Turn dough out onto a board or pastry cloth coated with about ¼ cup flour. Knead until dough is smooth and satiny and small bubbles form just under surface (10 to 12 minutes), adding just enough additional flour to prevent dough from being sticky.

3. Turn dough in a greased bowl. Cover and let rise in a warm place until doubled in bulk (35 to 45 minutes). Punch dough down, cover with inverted bowl, and let rest for 10 minutes.

Nippy Whipped Cream In a large bowl combine cream, lemon juice, mustard, salt, and white pepper. Beat until stiff. Fold in horseradish.

Makes about 2 cups.

ROAST CHICKEN IN HERB BREAD

This fat, herb-seasoned loaf of country bread holds a whole roast chicken. A lemony garlic butter seasons the chicken and the hollowed-out loaf. The bread can be baked a day in advance of serving and reheated during the last quarter hour the chicken roasts.

> 2 packages active dry yeast
> 2½ cups warm (105° to 115° F) water
> 1 tablespoon honey
> 1 teaspoon poultry seasoning
> 2 teaspoons salt
> 7 to 7½ cups unbleached all-purpose flour
> 1 egg white, beaten with 1 teaspoon water
> 2 teaspoons sesame seed
> 1 whole frying chicken (3 to 3½ lbs)
> 3 tablespoons butter or margarine
> 2 tablespoons olive oil
> 1 tablespoon lemon juice
> 1 clove garlic, minced or pressed

1. Sprinkle yeast over ½ cup of the warm water in large electric mixer bowl. Add honey. Let stand until yeast is soft (about 5 minutes).

2. Stir in remaining 2 cups warm water, poultry seasoning, and salt. Add 4½ cups of the flour. Mix to blend, then beat at medium speed until smooth and elastic (about 5 minutes). Stir in about 2 cups more flour to make a soft dough.

3. Turn dough out onto a coated board or pastry cloth. Knead until small bubbles form just under surface (20 to 25 minutes). Add just enough flour to keep dough from sticking.

4. Turn dough in a greased bowl. Cover with plastic wrap and a towel; let rise in a warm place until doubled in bulk (45 minutes to 1 hour).

5. Punch risen dough down; cover and let rest for 10 minutes. Shape dough into a stubby oval loaf about 10 inches long and 6 inches wide, tapering ends slightly.

6. Place on a greased baking sheet. Let rise until almost doubled in bulk (30 to 45 minutes). Brush loaf lightly with egg white mixture; sprinkle with sesame seed. Preheat oven to 375° F.

7. Bake until loaf is well browned and sounds hollow when tapped (45 to 55 minutes). Slide onto a wire rack and let cool for at least 2 hours.

8. About 2 hours before serving, remove chicken giblets (reserve, if you wish, for another use) and pull off and discard excess fat. In a small pan over medium heat, melt butter with olive oil, lemon juice, and garlic; bring to a boil and let boil for 2 minutes. Remove from heat. Brush chicken, inside and out, with butter mixture (reserve 2 to 3 tablespoons).

9. Preheat oven to 375° F. Place chicken on a rack in a shallow pan with wings tucked under and legs skewered or tied together. Roast, uncovered, until chicken is well browned and a leg moves freely when wiggled (about 1 hour and 30 minutes).

10. While chicken roasts, use a serrated knife to cut off top of loaf. With a curved knife, cut around edge to remove inside of bread (leave about a ¾-inch-thick crust). Reserve removed bread; use to make poultry stuffing or bread crumbs. Cut away some of the soft bread on underside of top of loaf. Brush inside of loaf (upper and lower parts) with reserved butter, oil, and garlic mixture.

11. Replace top and place loaf on a baking sheet in oven with chicken during last 15 minutes it roasts.

12. To serve, place chicken inside loaf. Replace top of loaf or stand it at a jaunty angle beside loaf and serve on a wooden board. Carve chicken, then slice bread shell into chunks. Serve hot or warm.

Serves 4.

A plump country loaf makes an edible serving container for roast chicken flavored with a lemony garlic butter.

INDEX

Note: Page numbers in italics refer to illustrations separated from recipe text.

U.S. MEASURE AND METRIC MEASURE CONVERSION CHART

		Formulas for Exact Measures			**Rounded Measures for Quick Reference**		
	Symbol	**When you know:**	**Multiply by**	**To find:**			
Mass (Weight)	oz	ounces	28.35	grams	1 oz		= 30 g
	lb	pounds	0.45	kilograms	4 oz		= 115 g
	g	grams	0.035	ounces	8 oz		= 225 g
	kg	kilograms	2.2	pounds	16 oz	= 1 lb	= 450 g
					32 oz	= 2 lb	= 900 g
					36 oz	= 2¼ lb	= 1,000 g (1 kg)
Volume	tsp	teaspoons	5.0	milliliters	¼ tsp	= 1/24 oz	= 1 ml
	tbsp	tablespoons	15.0	milliliters	½ tsp	= 1/12 oz	= 2 ml
	fl oz	fluid ounces	29.57	milliliters	1 tsp	= 1/6 oz	= 5 ml
	c	cups	0.24	liters	1 tbsp	= ½ oz	= 15 ml
	pt	pints	0.47	liters	1 c	= 8 oz	= 250 ml
	qt	quarts	0.95	liters	2 c (1 pt)	= 16 oz	= 500 ml
	gal	gallons	3.785	liters	4 c (1 qt)	= 32 oz	= 1 l.
	ml	milliliters	0.034	fluid ounces	4 qt (1 gal)	= 128 oz	= 3¾ l.
Length	in.	inches	2.54	centimeters	⅜ in.	= 1 cm	
	ft	feet	30.48	centimeters	1 in.	= 2.5 cm	
	yd	yards	0.9144	meters	2 in.	= 5 cm	
	mi	miles	1.609	kilometers	2½ in.	= 6.5 cm	
	km	kilometers	0.621	miles	12 in. (1 ft)	= 30 cm	
	m	meters	1.094	yards	1 yd	= 90 cm	
	cm	centimeters	0.39	inches	100 ft	= 30 m	
					1 mi	= 1.6 km	
Temperature	° F	Fahrenheit	5/9 (after subtracting 32)	Celsius	32° F	= 0° C	
					68 °F	= 20° C	
	° C	Celsius	9/5 (then add 32)	Fahrenheit	212° F	= 100° C	
Area	in.^{2}	square inches	6.452	square centimeters	1 in.^{2}	= 6.5 cm^2	
	ft^2	square feet	929.0	square centimeters	1 ft^2	= 930 cm^2	
	yd^2	square yards	8,361.0	square centimeters	1 yd^2	= 8,360 cm^2	
	a	acres	0.4047	hectares	1 a	= 4,050 m^2	